"Most business books give the [...] moment', maybe two. This one ke[...] after chapter. You won't be able [...] you'll immediately want to read it again."

—Matthew Pollard, bestselling author of
The Introvert's Edge series

"Megan is the real deal. The roadmap she provides in She Sells is refreshing and gives the reader all the keys they need for success. She's removed the blind spots and made the sales process less intimidating. Best yet, I can tell you she practices everything she preaches."

—Jerry Ghionis, World-Renowned Wedding Photographer, Nikon Ambassador & Double Grand Master of WPPI

"Finally, a great business book written from a woman's perspective! Selling shouldn't feel scary or uncomfortable, and after you read She Sells, it never will again. Megan shows that your ideal customers are all around you, and they can't wait for you to sell them their story."

—Heather Christie, JD, CSP, President of Evolve Global

She Sells

THE EMPATHY ADVANTAGE

How to Increase Profits and Give Clients What They Really Want

MEGAN DIPIERO

Elevation Publications
11523 Palmbrush Tr., Ste. 333
Lakewood Ranch, FL. 34202

Book cover and interior design by Monkey C Media
Cover photos by Jessi Norvell, Megan DiPiero Photography
Edited by Aric DiPiero

First Edition
Printed in the United States of America

ISBN: 978-1-7376480-1-7 (hardcover)
978-1-7376480-0-0 (trade)
978-1-7376480-2-4 (ebook)

Library of Congress Control Number: 2021916250

To the daughters of my readers:
Your mom has worked hard to shape her life and yours.
When we rise to the top, we make the world better.

CONTENTS

1 | WHAT BUSINESS ARE YOU REALLY IN?

What if I gave you permission to triple your prices tomorrow and guaranteed it would work?

Sit with that for a minute.

Whatever objection just popped into your head, table it for now.

I'll ask you this question again at the end of the book.

* * *

I started a photography business in Fort Myers, Florida. Take away the non-stop sunshine and clear blue skies and this city is probably a lot like yours. There are good neighborhoods and bad. We're known for our beaches, but guess what? There are plenty of strip malls and cow fields here too. What's more, the median household income for my city is only about half the national average. Not exactly a luxury market.

That wasn't my only limitation. I launched my business right after the Great Recession, in a starter home on the wrong side of town. My clients had to drive up to an hour to reach me, overlooking unkempt lawns and toppled trash cans along the way. Why did they do it? Because they knew I was the girl who had the goods.

My last year in that humble home studio my average client spent over $5,000, and I did $400,000 in total revenue—both figures easily ten times higher than the majority of photographers in my area. I now operate out of a 700-square-foot commercial space in a nearly-deserted mall, and have increased my client average and annual revenue by another 50%.

So what's my secret?

Even though the name on the door says Megan DiPiero Photography, I am not a photographer.

If I ran a catering company, I wouldn't be a chef.

If I owned a high-end beauty salon, I wouldn't be a stylist.

No matter what business you're in and no matter what market you serve, if you want to be wildly successful you need to set aside your pre-conceived idea that your profession is your role.

At times I'm a marriage counselor. I'm usually a therapist. I'm often an interior designer and a gracious concierge. Above all, I'm a friend and a listening ear. I fulfill all of these roles, yet when my clients write me a check the subject line says "for photography."

What my clients find, and the reason why I have such a strong repeat and referral base, is that they don't need me for photos. Sure, that might be what prompts them to pick up the phone. But the real reason they say yes to booking is that they need confidence. They need validation. They need me to relieve their anxiety. They need empowerment. They need to honor what's most special to them.

These portraits they crave? The product is really just a souvenir of that experience.

When you evolve beyond your job description and embrace your empathy advantage, you no longer have any competition. You've created a space all your own—free from comparison and constraint. Better yet, the more you charge, the more your clients will value what you have to offer. But I'm getting ahead of myself.

Let me show you what I mean with this true story.

The Time I Stole a Sale

Years ago, I saw a post online that read: "Photog friends! Anyone available for a shoot March 18? I'm booked that day. But if you share your contact info below, I'll pass it along."

I think most of my fellow pros would have assumed this was another run-of-the-mill, in-and-out family affair—some price shopper on the hunt for a "reasonable photographer." In our field, "reasonable" usually translates to around $250 for an hour or two of shooting. Clients expect you'll hand over the digital files lightly retouched and call it a day. That's probably what the original poster had in mind, and I'm guessing everyone on the thread jumped to the same conclusion.

By the time I read it, a half-dozen other photographers had already commented "I'm free!" and linked their websites or Instas.

Never one to be deterred by competition, I also threw my hat in the ring. At the time, I found it odd I was the only person who gave out their phone number. I wondered, *What's up with that?*

The next day, the prospect called. I answered on the second ring.

"Oh thank God you picked up." I could hear the frustration in her voice. Turns out, my lead's name was Amy.[1] She'd spent the previous day stalking websites from her provided list, hunting down phone numbers and emailing in vain. Not a soul had bothered to connect. I was the first.

Let the empathy begin.

"Man, that's frustrating. I'm here for you, Amy. How can I help?"

Already, she understood I was on her side. Feeling heard, Amy returned to the business at hand. Her prepared questions followed:

- *Was I available on March 18th?*

- *Did I do beach portraits?*

- *How much would all this cost?*

I imagine when you get a phone call or an email from a prospect of your own, it's probably along the same lines: "Can you do [the thing]? Can you fit my time and budget?"

Those are every prospect's questions because that's all they know to ask—the surface-level stuff. If what I sold was professional photography, I would have simply answered.

But remember: I don't sell photography.

Not really.

Instead, I said, "You got it, Amy! I'll be happy to tell you everything you need to know! But is it okay if I ask you a couple questions first

---

1 Well, actually, that wasn't her name. My policy is to never kiss-and-tell, so the names and details of the clients mentioned throughout this book have all been changed.

so I can better understand what you're looking for? First up, tell me who we'll be photographing?"

She quickly counted them off: her husband and their two kids, her brother and his two kids, her mom and dad, and their family friends.

"Family friends? Huh. You guys must be really close."

Turns out "close" was an understatement. The two families vacationed together every year. Their kids were inseparable. They had both become part of the other's family.

"This year is going to be a little different though." Amy's voice dropped low. "Jason passed away unexpectedly. He was my brother's best friend. And my kids' favorite uncle. Well, they called him uncle anyway..." Her voice trailed off. "It's going to feel so different without him."

I told her how sorry I was and left some room for the heaviness in the air to pass. When she was ready, I gently said, "Talk to me about the beach you have in mind."

"Well, it needs to be a short beach."

A "short beach," I thought. What in the world is a "short beach?"

Out loud, I said, "Tell me a little bit more about that."

"So, my dad has mobility issues and sometimes it takes a while to get out to the water. I'm just worried about how far he'll have to walk."

Oh! A short walk *to* the beach. Got it.

I brainstormed some ideas to offer solutions. All the location scouting I'd done in the past came to the rescue. There was a private beach I knew of that would fit the bill for a "short beach." And another came to mind that had beach wheelchairs, the kind with big, puffy plastic wheels. Plus, I'd just networked with the owner at a prop rental company, and I was sure I could get my hands on some great chairs so that her father could be comfortably seated yet still dignified throughout the shoot.

"That's such a relief." Amy confessed. "My dad's a proud man and he's not doing real well with all of this."

"All of this...?"

The line went silent. For a second, I wondered if Amy's call had cut out. Just when I was about to chime in, she breathed deeply, and I sensed something big was coming. "Yeah. Late-stage Parkinson's. It's not good. We planned this trip because we don't know if he'll be with us next year."

When I heard these words, the hair on the back of my arms stood up. It suddenly hit me this wasn't just any old beach shoot. I immediately thought of my own dad and my own two kids. To think my kids may only have him for one last year. My every thought was now focused on honoring this moment for them.

Quietly, I said, "Amy, my heart goes out to you. I can tell that this is going to be the most important shoot that we do all year."

Almost in a whisper, she said, "Thank you, Megan. I think so, too."

Time out.

Let's pause the story for a moment to talk. In general, the sales profession tends to get a bad rap. And this is a book all about sales. So I have to ask you, having read this far, what are your reactions?

Does any part of this feel icky? Manipulative? Sleazy?

Or does it feel caring, connected, collaborative?

So far, I've let Amy have the stage while I acted as a listening ear and helped draw out her hopes, her dreams, and her needs. My head and heart are always in the problem-solving space. As more information unfolded, I used my expertise to guide Amy toward the solutions she craved.

WHAT IF EVERY SALE COULD JUST BE A CONVERSATION BETWEEN FRIENDS?

What if every sale could just be a conversation between friends?

Spoiler alert! With the proper business model, it can!

We went on to talk about the remaining details and logistics. Now that I understood the scope of the job, I knew I wanted to bring in a second shooter. We could divide and conquer and get all the shot variety we wanted before the little kids grew restless. Plus, I knew Amy would want to get back to her family time and their vacation together.

Last and certainly not least, I wanted to know: "How would you like to enjoy all these beautiful portraits? Are you guys wall art fans? Or album fans?"

"Both!"

I could hear her smiling.

Amy loved the idea of buying wall art and albums for everyone as gifts. She was happy to foot the bill and treat her loved ones to something special.

We were nearing the end of the call, but I felt there was still something missing. "Amy, I want to acknowledge that this is the first year your whole family won't all be together. What if we created a memorial page for Jason in the family albums?"

"Oh my god, Megan—could you do that? I mean, all we really have of him is a cell phone picture."

I couldn't imagine. Being so close to someone and only having a selfie to remember them by.

But thank goodness for the wonders of modern technology: "Don't worry," I said. "Leave it to me. Whatever you can get your hands on, I'll work my magic and make it look as beautiful as the portraits we create together."

The mood on the call had become one of celebration and excitement. We were 180 degrees from where we'd started. I could feel Amy's anxiety lifting and that her stress and fears surrounding this day had all been replaced by hope. Not hope that I could somehow make all of this tragedy disappear but hope that someone understood how much this meant—that someone would honor these moments with her. That we could work as a team to create something beautiful and meaningful.

And now, finally...back to Amy's first questions when we started the call. Could I handle her portrait needs? Without a doubt! What was this shoot going to cost her? In the end, she didn't bat an eye at the grand total of $16,000. In fact, she was excited.

Joyful!

Grateful.

And oh! What about the third question she had? The question that actually launched that online referral thread so many days ago. Was I available March 18th?

"Ummm...Amy, there's just one thing. I know you were looking for a photographer on the 18th. I'm actually booked up on that date. I will move heaven and earth to shift things around if needed. But is there any chance you guys can shoot the day before or after?"

"Of course! Not a problem, Megan! We're there all week."

"Great! I can't wait to meet you all!"

So about that sale—did I steal it? Or did I earn it?

I was the seventh service provider Amy reached out to. Eighth, if we're including the original poster who was so quick to refer it out.

They say customer service is dead. And it shows.

Even if we give the other businesses the benefit of the doubt—let's say the photographer third in line emailed back pricing and photographer #4 made contact via text—they still wouldn't have given Amy what she really deserved: true connection, real empathy, and solutions beyond the surface.

Sell Me My Story

Here's the big lie you've been told your whole life: People don't like spending money.

Sure, no one enjoys overpaying for something routine. If you've ever been on Amazon and seen the exact same product—same brand and everything—offered by two different sellers and one is charging three times as much, you roll your eyes and add the lower-priced option to your cart. But when it comes to something *meaningful*, a whole different thought process kicks in.

Try this experiment with me. Think back to the biggest purchases you've made over the past five to ten years. Stretch your memory until you find that breakthrough point. We're looking for outliers that are above and beyond your normal range of spending.

Need some ideas?

What big vacations come to mind? Did you splurge on someone you love? Did you treat yourself to any material goods, like a new wardrobe? Jewelry? Fine art? Dream car? How about home purchases or renovations? A time-share or lakeside cottage? What about personal advancement? A business coach? Tools of the trade? Studio upgrade? Did you recently celebrate a milestone life event? Wedding? New baby? Twentieth anniversary?

Do not read on until you have at least one big purchase firmly in mind.

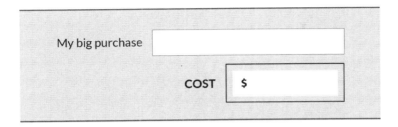

Now answer these follow-up questions:

- *Why did you make that big purchase?*
- *How did you justify it to yourself?*
- *What value did it bring into your life?*
- *How do you feel about that purchase years later?*

Spending money—especially big, impactful money—becomes a touchstone in our lives. We can conjure up the experience in our imagination for years to come.

Of the thousands of students in my coaching business who I've posed this question to over the years, everyone can list at least one monumental purchase. And here's the fascinating part: These purchases are all different and unique based on what the individual values.

You might find the way I spend to be absurd. We send our kids to a private Montessori school to the tune of $30,000 a year. Yes, even in my business start-up years, our family spent as much as one quarter of our annual income sending our kids to school. Now is the time when people usually like to remind me that public school is free.

I spent $25,000 on our bucket-list twentieth anniversary destination photo shoot. And yet ironically, I'm not even sporting a wedding ring in a single photo. Haven't worn one in decades. Look at your ring right now. I promise you it costs more than mine. Jewelry just isn't my thing. I think it's silly to spend on such frivolity. But portraits? No price is too high!

I have friends who would mortgage their house to buy a horse.

I've seen students spend $50,000 on life coaching.

I have a family member whose splurge every few years is hunting big game in Africa, and here's me—the vegan—just scratching my head.

The thing is, you don't have to value what I value and vice versa. When we look at the purchase examples above, people are buying big for one very important reason: They are purchasing a piece of their identity.

That Tesla on your vision board isn't there because you need transportation from point A to point B. It's about telling the world, "I've arrived. I've achieved it." The rock on your ring finger says, "I'm in a loving relationship and my spouse would give anything to make me smile." That gear in your camera bag is the commitment you made to yourself when you said, "I believe in this dream."

Every big purchase I've ever made over my life has shaped who I am, and I don't regret any of them. Who am I to deprive my client of this meaning-making experience?

Should Amy have spent $16,000 on a family photo shoot? Was it really worth it? It doesn't matter what I think or what anyone else thinks. What matters is that it was worth it to Amy. This was her way of saying to herself and to the world, *"This is how much my family means to me. These are the relationships I honor."* Our

PEOPLE BUY BIG FOR ONE VERY IMPORTANT **REASON:** THEY ARE PURCHASING A **PIECE** OF THEIR **IDENTITY.**

experience together has now become an indelible part of her story, and those treasured products I designed for her are her souvenirs.

Want to provide a product or service that can change someone's life? It starts with raising your prices.

2 | PRICE SIGNALS WORTH

Have you ever experienced a disconnect between what you expected something to cost and what it actually cost? I have this experience all the time. When I see a product or service that's priced higher than I expect, I lean in and get curious. *What don't I know about this? Maybe it's more valuable than I assumed?*

When I see someone under-charging, I can't keep my mouth shut. I'm Team Price Hike! I always want to root people on to get them charging what they're worth. Perfect example coming atcha! During my pregnancy and stay-at-home mom days, I was what you'd call a crunchy granola mama. For our first birth, we planned to avoid the hospital entirely and set our hearts and our minds on a home waterbirth instead. Right now, you're either totally rolling your eyes at me or you're jumping up and down to have found a kindred spirit.

(To my soul sisters, ask me to tell you about the time I gave birth at The Farm! Everyone else, just keep reading.)

Birthing babies was certainly not my area of expertise, so of course I hired some capable guides to help me along the way. We enlisted the services of a homebirth midwife and a doula named Amanda. For those of you unfamiliar with this term, doula is just a fancy name for a birth coach. But Amanda was so much more than that. She turned out to be an invaluable resource. Not only did she know her stuff professionally, she also became a family friend over all the months we worked together.

When it finally came time to pay Amanda's fee, we were shocked at her rate. What did she charge for all her time, care, and expertise? Just $500. We weren't having it. She deserved so much more. My husband Aric and I decided to triple her pay to $1,500 and wouldn't take no for an answer. We told her that we could afford it and wanted her to be able to keep providing her exceptional service to others.

Have you ever had a client nudge you to raise your rates? It's always an eye-opening experience when it happens. If clients and colleagues are telling you that you're priced too low, listen up!

Maybe the only thing holding you back...is you.

Doesn't It Feel Good to Pay More?

Sometimes even established brands need this wake-up call.

In 2018, the struggling discount chain Payless Shoe Source came up with a clever ad concept. The premise: to expose the overpriced fashion industry with a revealing social experiment. If their plan worked out, not only would they win points for taking a jab at luxury brands, but they'd also reassure their down-to-earth customer base that they were wise and savvy shoppers.

To set the stage, Payless leased a former Armani store in an upscale Santa Monica mall and paid an ad agency millions to convert it into a fake luxury brand called...wait for it...*Palessi*. No detail was overlooked in the transformation. Picture glowing glass display shelves and golden statues, plus avant-garde, branded art installations. A young, fashion-forward sales team was cast and trained for the launch.

And now for the most important detail of all: The shelves were stocked with their regular Payless inventory but instead of the usual price tags like $19.99 or $39.99, for Palessi they marked the footwear up as much as 1,800%. Would people really pay $200, $300, $500, or even more for shoes normally sold at a fraction the price?

Lights, Camera, Fashion!

Out rolled the red carpet and in came the unsuspecting grand-opening guests. While invited social media influencers and fashion-istas were entertained up front, the production team huddled backstage watching the experiment unfold through hidden cameras.

What happened next should have opened the eyes of every execu-tive back at HQ. To everyone's delight, their grand opening was a huge success! Go watch the magic unfold on YouTube for yourself. The customers were buying it! Those interviewed described the exquisite craftsmanship of the shoes, the versatility, the sophistica-tion. Remember, nothing had changed about the product quality—just the price tag and the experience.

One shopper said she might wear her new find to a Met Gala dinner. A young Italian designer gushed at how fortunate he was just to be able to experience the new brand. An edgy fashion critic raved Palessi was all about "taking your shoe game up to the next level." The register kept ringing and the customers kept smiling. A retailer's dream come true!

The cheers backstage, however, were for a different reason entirely. The folks watching on monitors exchanged high fives with each sale. Why were they celebrating? Not because their guests were thrilled. Not because Palessi was making bank that night. They were cheering because they'd pulled off their prank. Just one room over, people were actually overpaying for products and they'd captured the farce on camera! Wait until the internet saw this!

After enough sales had been rung up to prove their point, the producers called a halt to the experiment. The cameras kept rolling for the big reveal. Consumers were let in on the stunt, refunded their money, and given the shoes they had purchased as a gift.

The exit interviews that followed are actually kind of heart-wrenching. Those same people who had been glowing before—feeling as though they'd just bought an exciting piece of their personal stories—now had fallen faces. They didn't look angry. Just sad. Minutes ago, they had been sophisticated fashionistas taking part in the coolest party in town, imagining themselves on the red carpet, rubbing elbows with industry insiders...and now they were just gullible saps with no taste. One person almost resignedly said, "I am still happy with my purchase. Guess I'll be going to Payless now."

I highly doubt that.

So what were the takeaways? For Payless, they enjoyed a brief flurry of media attention and internet buzz. But if their intention had been to lure luxury shoppers into their unappealing and cramped discount stores, they never stood a chance.

The real answer to their problems was staring them in the face. For all the wrong reasons, they had actually stumbled upon a thriving business model with excited customers and great margins. Had they tuned in to the results of their own experiment, they might have seen an exciting new direction for their company. What they did instead was pat themselves on the back while they continued to cling to an outdated and failing discount model. The biggest gotcha moment in this story? Payless Shoe Source entered Chapter 11 bankruptcy three months later and ultimately closed all of its U.S. stores.

Expensive Wine Tastes Better

Was it simply the high ticket prices that got buyers excited at Palessi? Or was it the environment that turned their heads? A glittering showroom, party atmosphere, and dazzling people would be enough to make anyone feel carried away in the moment. What if all that was stripped away? How would price impact your reaction then?

One of the bonus perks of being a mom is that you can totally hunker down guilt-free for educational TV viewing with your kids and call it parenting, not procrastination. This is how I stumbled upon one of our family's faves: *Brain Games*. In season five, episode four, my ears perked up when I heard the opening title: "Money." This ought to be good!

In the show, they set up a simple street-side experiment. Two cakes are offered up for taste testing with the premise that participants' feedback will help the bakers with their market research. Cake #1, a creamy looking chocolate delight, was marked with a sign that said $15. Cake #2 was remarkably similar in appearance but with one obvious difference. Its sign read $55.

Taste-testers sampled and commented away. Cake #1 was judged as "dry" with "not enough frosting." Overall opinion: disappointing.

Then came Cake #2, the $55 cake. Immediately the spoken and non-verbal reactions shifted. Smacking lips, "Mmms" and "Ohhhs." Through stuffed mouths they declared the second option "delicious," "moister," "smoother," "richer." This one was hands down the crowd favorite.

You're probably wise to the experiment by now, so it likely won't shock you when I reveal that the two cakes were exactly the same. Same ingredients, same baker, cooked at the same time in the same oven. Why then were folks so easily swayed? Did the more expensive cake actually taste better?

Jonah Berger, Wharton School of University of Pennsylvania professor and best-selling business author, explained: "Your brain is always trying to make comparisons. Because our cake eaters thought they were eating different cakes their brains used the price points to influence enjoyment. Higher price is assumed to mean higher quality. And even thinking something is more expensive causes the part of your brain which is related to rewards to activate and actually cause you to enjoy it more."

Even after the reveal, some taste-testers still didn't believe they were hearing the truth. In their minds, the cakes really were vastly different. And one cake—the more expensive of the two—was the one they declared, "So much better!"

Ok, so in this experiment we've removed most of the variables... both cakes were presented in the exact same setting and only the price was different. But even still, this was a made-for-TV setup. Maybe the Taste-testers were influenced by the crowd and the cameras. Can we get even *more* scientific?

Dr. Antonio Rangel of the California Institute of Technology put our remaining concerns to rest by taking his research off the street and into the lab. Twenty subjects volunteered to have their brains scanned as part of his study. The activity of their medial orbitofrontal cortex—the area of the brain responsible for registering pleasant experiences—was measured while they were introduced to five different wines.

As with our cake eaters and shoe buyers, once again, there was some price fibbing and trickery at play. Though the participants thought they were sampling five unique wines, they were actually presented with only three—two had been served up twice with different prices. The prices of each wine were announced as participants sampled them. These ranged from $5 to $90 per bottle.

As the stated price per sip went up, so did their brain activity. *The Economist* reported "...when one of the wines was said to cost $10 a bottle it was rated less than half as good as when people were told it cost $90 a bottle, its true retail price." Did you catch that? Even though this was actually an expensive wine, people enjoyed it less when they were told it was cheap. When presented with the same wine twice at different price points, the participants experienced a difference in enjoyment levels. This effect vanished when they ran the study again without giving participants the pricing information. Price truly does affect perception. And to your brain, more expensive wine actually does taste better.

You want to bring value to your clients, right? You want them to feel that their purchase is meaningful. You want to honor their story and what matters to them. So, why do so many of us show our clients to the $10 wine when what they really want is the pleasure of that $90 indulgence?

PRICE TRULY DOES AFFECT PERCEPTION. TO YOUR BRAIN, MORE EXPENSIVE WINE ACTUALLY DOES TASTE BETTER.

Packaging Beats Perfection

Let's be honest. What's holding us back is fear that we're not ready.

I was raised to believe that success follows hard work. That dues paid translates into dollars earned. Picture a graph where skill is the X-axis and income is the Y-axis. What do you get? A straight-line trending upward, of course!

Conventional wisdom can be very comforting. It can also be misleading. Let's say you spend your whole career only perfecting your craft. Once it's clear you're the best around, will your audience then beat a path to your door with fistfuls of money? Let's find out.

In January 2007, *The Washington Post* arranged a stunt to test whether excellence would be inherently recognized. On a chilly January morning, they stationed Joshua Bell, one of the world's greatest virtuoso musicians, at one of the busiest D.C. metro stations—Washington's L'Enfant.

On that busy rush hour morning, thousands of bustling commuters were on their way to work. Little did they know the treat in store for them. Bell readied himself for his performance but first made sure to leave his open violin case at his feet, seeded with tip money just like any savvy street performer would do. From this case, he had drawn not just any violin but a $3.5 million-dollar 1713 Stradivari. The musician and the instrument were primed for a great performance.

Bow raised and mind focused, he began to play.

For the next forty-three minutes, Bell performed six classical pieces selected not for their familiarity but for their transcendent, timeless brilliance. You should go give it a listen online. Your heart

23

will break at both the sublime beauty and the astounding lack of appreciation and attention paid. More than a thousand people passed by during Bell's performance. Only a handful briefly stopped to listen. No appreciable crowd ever gathered.

And what money did this master make for his time and talent? Bell's tips totaled $32.17.

The question posed by the experiment had been: To what extent does context matter when evaluating talent?

As columnist Gene Weingarten of *The Washington Post* noted, here we had "...one of the finest classical musicians in the world, playing some of the most elegant music ever written on one of the most valuable violins ever made." And yet the beauty fell on deaf ears.

Put this same man in a hallowed concert hall, and he can command $1,000 a minute. But in these humble surroundings, everyone just hears another starving artist trying to make ends meet.

Packaging matters.

Ask for loose change and your work will be judged accordingly. Command attention from your audience by setting prices that make them sit up and take notice, then watch how perception and gratitude shift.

But Am I Ready?

The clear solution is to raise your prices.

You can see now that that's the answer. Our brains tell us higher price tags equal more value. Literally. Your clients appreciate spending more. Surely you will appreciate receiving more. But I know that simply raising your rates is a lot easier said than done.

Before we move forward, we've got to deal with that stifling fear that's filling you with doubt and dread. Have you worried over thoughts like these?

- *"I'm not ready to charge more yet because my work just isn't good enough."*
- *"I can't move forward until I've mastered my craft."*
- *"There's another artist in my market whose work is better than mine, and she charges less than I do already!"*
- *"I haven't paid my dues."*
- *"I'm not worth it."*

I run a Facebook group for professional photographers where we talk business, pricing, and sales. We have business owners at every level, from just starting to veteran pros earning well into the six-figures. Ready to have your mind blown? Sometimes the newbies have better art than the big earners who've been around the block. Sales average is not necessarily contingent on mastery of art.

Don't get me wrong. I'm not advocating that you go out and sell garbage and call it gold. As someone with great empathy, I know that's not in your makeup to rip folks off. Let's agree that you should have a baseline skill level to go into business. You must have competency to call yourself a pro. But beyond that, the truth of what makes a master can be a bit subjective.

Remember: the $55-dollar cake and the $15-dollar cake were the exact same cake. But the $15 sample was declared a disappointment by those who tasted it, and the $55 version won rave reviews. The baker in that hypothetical example might have felt unworthy of charging $55. Maybe she had tasted better cakes before. Maybe she knew she would have more baking skill a year from now. But had she caved and gone to market with the humble price, the response from her customers would have been a self-fulfilling prophecy. Dry, not enough frosting. About what you'd expect for $15. By instead opting for the higher price, she would give customers permission to appreciate her work, and in the end both she and they would have a more rewarding experience.

If you're ready to charge at all—if people are already paying you for your work—that tells me you have a viable product or service.

Congratulations! You are ready to charge big!

Go ahead and charge that meaningful, joy-enhancing rate!

Best of all, when you escape the trap of starving artist, you can ensure you'll survive long enough to actually achieve the mastery you seek. We all want to get to Joshua Bell-level brilliance. I don't know a single artist worth her salt who's shrugged and said, *"You know what? This is good enough. I'll stop learning now."* Nonsense. We grow day by day. Year by year. I've been in professional sales for twenty five-plus years and I've been a professional photographer for over a decade. I'm still mastering both crafts. Had I waited till that elusive "master level" to start charging, I'd have hung it up long ago. If you want to be in business long enough to reach the high levels of the pros you admire most, you'll stay in the game with us.

Your work is good enough.

You are good enough.

Right now.

What Clients Really Want

Ok, let's recap what we've talked about so far.

In telling you the story of Amy's beach shoot, I showed that there are opportunities for big sales all around us, if we only take the time to explore our clients' deeper needs. And it's up to us to draw this out of them.

Next, I suggested that, deep down, clients want to spend meaningful money on purchases that help them tell their own story. The decision to pull the trigger on those scary purchases becomes a touchstone in their lives and lets them define the person they are going forward.

In the anecdotes and studies that followed, I demonstrated that packaging and presentation matter *a lot* to our buyers. Depending on the setting, even sophisticated buyers could mistake a Payless shoe for a designer piece or (in the reverse) a renowned virtuoso for a street performer.

In short, customers who have been primed to expect an amazing experience are enthusiastic and committed. Those whose expectations have been lowered tend to be more critical and disappointed. Your pricing is the first—and maybe the most powerful—signal that tells their brain how to interpret what is coming next.

All good news for entrepreneurs!

Price high. Delight your client. Everyone wins!

"But wait," your empathetic heart nudges. "If I raise my rates, won't I shut out all those clients who love my business as-is?"

Our empathy calls us to be kind and considerate. We want to provide for everyone, not just the jet set mansion-dwellers.

"What about our friends and family...regular folks like us?"

Before you get too worried that you're excluding an entire market segment, I have reassuring news! You can move forward, embrace the big bucks, and ***still*** continue to serve clients from every walk of life.

Let's talk about how people spend money today.

Time to catch you up with the modern consumer.

3 | SECRETS OF THE NEW ECONOMY

Knock, knock, Neo.

The Matrix. Best movie of the 90s! *Best movie ever?*

Back in the spring of '99, my soon-to-be husband, Aric, drove halfway across the country to my college dorm with one expressed mission: take me out on an epic movie date and have the time of our lives!

Well, I said one *expressed* mission. Little did I know there were other plans in store, namely a surprise proposal! But let's not let that engagement overshadow the drama of big screen kung fu and badass Agent Smith, bullet-time camera moves, and bullet-dodging superheroes.

I told you...Best. Movie. Ever!

As this was my third *Matrix* viewing in theaters and Aric's twelfth (!), we figured we ought to do it up. Aric donned his floor-sweeping black duster with mirrored sunglasses, and I paired an oil-black vinyl bodysuit with pleather jeans. (We take our movie watching *very* seriously!) Seven friends squeezed into my five-seater sports car and we raced to our showtime, blasting the soundtrack the whole way there.

Why did this movie strike such a chord with rebellious thinkers the world over?

The moral of the story, as any *Matrix* fan can tell you, is that you must free your mind. When Neo's hero Morpheus presented that red pill, Neo was finally able to see the world for what it was. Who can forget that feeling of revulsion and betrayal when the main character and the moviegoing audience realized how blind we were to reality? Through mind-bending training and with the help of his fellow believers, Neo was able to let go of the world he knew and fight for the world he wanted. He discovered anything was possible if he just believed in himself. He could rewrite the rules. There is no spoon.

Fortunately, our world is not as bleak as Neo's. There are no squiddies coming to attack us. There are no body-snatching agents to be feared. But there are some similarities between his journey and ours. If we really want to thrive as entrepreneurs, we need to see things as they truly are and release our outdated preconceptions about the way things work.

While we've been punching the clock and eating our Tasty Wheat, the U.S. economy has been shifting. Take this red pill and I'll show you how deep the rabbit hole goes.

The Three Spending Lanes

To know where we're going, we have to see where we've been.

Let's explore a familiar idea we likely all have experience with—back-to-school shopping. Specifically, I want you to cast your mind back to shopping in the eighties. Not born yet? Go ask your mom! Everyone else, join me on a trip down memory lane.

Were you a mall shopper? A mart shopper? Or a money-is-no-object shopper? The answer likely depends on what income your family made.

Let's say your family was middle class. Where did you shop? The mall of course! Sears, a popular mall anchor, was the number one retailer in America all throughout the eighties. Stores like Gap, The Limited, and Thom McAn were fixtures of most American malls and middle-class lifestyles. Middle class families paid **mid-tier** prices for *middle of the road* service and *mid-range* quality. It was the Goldilocks tale of shopping—not too high, not too low, just right!

What if your family was having a hard time making ends meet? Your shopping experience would be quite different. You likely gravitated toward one of the big value mart chains—Kmart, Walmart, or other discount retailers. The focus here was on getting a great **value**. At the big box stores, quality, style, and service were nothing to write home about but hey, the price point was great! And as the Fresh Prince of Bel Air's mom would remind us in "Parents Just Don't Understand": *"You go to school to learn, not for a fashion show."*

Now, let's say you were a richy-rich! Lucky you! You skipped the value and mid-market brands completely and chose **luxury** for your shopping experience. Growing up in Jersey, I heard legends of girls who would shop at Bloomingdales in swanky Short Hills. They might even drive into the City to hit up the boutiques. There, they would be spoiled with hands-on customer care and attention. Service, fashion, and experience were all elevated. And so were the price points! For the wealthy elite, money was no object and back-to-school shopping, like all purchases, tended to stay on the pricier end.

What was happening here? What were the market forces at work?

Back in the day, buyers tended to stay in their lanes. Imagine a highway with bold, solid lines marking off your path. Could you cross lanes? Yes. But for the most part, people stayed where class and social convention prescribed.

The three spending lanes looked like this:

Earn a lot, indulge a lot: We have a lane for you! Earn a little, spend a little: Here's your lane right over here! Social pressure stigmatized switching lanes. We were kept in check and influenced not to reach too high or drop too low. As a middle-class junior high kid, I would have been just as mercilessly teased if I showed up to school in a Gucci shirt as I would have dressed head-to-toe in consignment clothes. The message came across loud and clear: Stay in your lane.

And then in the 1990s, three big changes hit the retail landscape all around the same time. Warning: Road Construction Ahead! Our three-lane spending highway was about to experience an overhaul.

Rise of the Discount Giants

While malls were cashing in on the middle class, Walmart spent years systematically perfecting their distribution network. They pioneered and launched the Supercenter concept in 1988 and began furiously expanding across the United States. Though not as much of an experience as the mall and with a little less handholding and panache, the roll-back Walmart prices commanded attention. Promising ultimate convenience, incredible savings, and good (though not exceptional) products and services, Walmart began to turn the heads of middle-class consumers. In 1991, for the first time in decades, mid-market superstar Sears was unseated as the largest retailer in the United States. The new champion? Wally World!

That was the first jab thrown at the institution of the American shopping mall. Target landed the second.

Remember back when Target became "Tar-zhay?" The first time I heard it referred to this way, I thought my friends were joking.

Target? The big box store with the discount buys? When did they become fancy?

It turned out Target was bringing cheap chic fashion onto the scene. Their marketing efforts aimed to eliminate the stigma of shopping at value stores. Designer brands created exclusive lines for them. Merchandising and advertising projected a new, hip vibe. Target's stores started to feel less like discount warehouses and a lot more clean, inviting, and approachable.

But the nineties weren't done yet. A third disruptor was about to enter the ring and serve up the ultimate mid-market knockout blow. Coming in like a kitten but poised for a mighty roar...presenting: The Internet!

The birth of Amazon in 1994 caused immediate trauma to brick-and-mortar booksellers. I managed an independent bookstore in the late nineties and felt the impact first-hand. It was a tough beat for those of us in the industry. While shoppers were saddened to see their neighborhood booksellers struggle, they also found it hard to resist the massive variety and ease of shopping online.

Back then, people couldn't have imagined the powerhouse that e-commerce would eventually become. In the decades that followed, the "Amazon effect" would take hold in every product category.

Changing Lanes

The solid lines of our three steadfast buying lanes, once so rigid and well-defined, began to blur. It had suddenly become okay for affluent consumers to score a cheap fashion find at Target. Could this power to choose go both ways? If the upper class could swerve into the value lane, was it possible that the middle and lower classes could also turn on their blinkers and head for the luxury lane?

Earlier, I asked you to identify a time when you made a big, dreamy purchase—reaching well outside your norm and appreciating every dollar spent. Let me tell you the tale of two wide-eyed kids and how one ginormous purchase forever shaped the way I see buying and selling in our modern economy.

The year: 2006. My movie-loving man and I found ourselves endlessly in love and now living in our affordable first home on the outskirts of town. The operative word here? *Affordable.* With the birth of baby boy Koan, we dropped from two incomes to one and decidedly tightened our belts a notch or two. I claimed the role of stay-at-home mom. And Aric went out to win that bread for the family.

Important to note: Up to this point in our lives, Aric and I had been rather frugal. Our elopement wedding cost only a couple hundred dollars. Our idea of a grand date night back then was watching movies at home. We were both raised lower-middle class and weren't what you would call lavish spenders. Little did we know when we made our house a home that our no-frills bedroom suite would become the site of one of our most expensive and extravagant family purchases to date.

When you picture a starter home, you likely imagine bare-bones functionality and builder-grade fixtures. Ours was no different. There was one detail in particular that used to drive me crazy—our bedroom had these annoying sliding mirrored doors. Aesthetically, I found them tacky. Functionally, I found them inconvenient. Now, try adding a cruising baby to the scene and watch the problems multiply. Imagine the never-ending fingerprints. The mewing trapped cat. (It happens!) The fearful crashes when little guy puts his curiosity to slide and *SLAM!* to the test.

Did I need a better closet solution? Yes! But more than simply form and function, what I really craved as a sleep-deprived new mom was the hope of beginning each day with order and beauty. I missed getting dressed up for work and putting on pretty things. I missed my organized lifestyle and clean surfaces. I wanted to return to morning routines of calm and zen. And not to mention, I was a grown-up now. I had a husband, home, and happy baby. I wanted to feel like I had *arrived*. That was my dream.

"Let's just see what California Closets would cost," Aric suggested. "It's not like we have to buy anything."

The salesperson drove nearly an hour to reach us—past construction and cow fields. She must have been wondering where the GPS was taking her, but she never spoke a word of doubt or called our commitment into question. From moment one, she treated us like we belonged. I had never experienced a luxury sale before. I was awed by the level of care and attention I received. Here I was, a stay-at-home mom in an out-of-bounds neighborhood that, I'm sure, she'd never been to before or since, and yet she acted like I was her VIP. A taste of the country club way out in the country!

And not only was the *experience* everything I craved, the *products* were top notch, too. I was presented with polished drawer pulls, 3D renderings, vision boards, and wood door finish samples that were decidedly NOT mirrored.

After I had fallen completely in love with the concept and the company, my salesperson presented the price tag. A jaw-dropping $10,000. Yeah, I felt like throwing up. We didn't have that kind of money sitting around. How in the world could I possibly justify spending that much? We couldn't afford it. Out of the question. What would our middle-class parents and friends say?

But I wanted it.

Man, I *really* wanted it.

Somehow, this single-income couple found a way to make it happen. We scrimped and saved and maxed out a couple of credit cards. My heart melted when Aric said, "You deserve this. Happy Mother's Day!"

Did I win the husband lottery or what!?

There was no way to rationally explain why we did what we did. But the desire was there, the solution was made clear, and where there's a will to trade up, there's a way.

That's the thing about buying meaning, about selling someone their story. That closet was a defining purchase in my life, a milemarker on my journey. Would off-the-rack Closet Maid storage have done the trick? Sure! But because we bought something that really *meant something*, it had a huge emotional impact on me that's stayed with me to this day.

Trading Up, Trading Down

Middle class. Middle means. BIG dreams.

In the 1980s, purchases like this for a family like mine would have been a true anomaly. Back then, custom closets were for the wealthy upper class—out of sight and out of reach for most others.

But now, in the twenty-first century, buying looks quite different. Through the phenomenon called "trading up, trading down," consumers and marketers continue to reshape the buying landscape.

What happens today when a commodity or service holds little value to us? We trade down. Trading down is reserved for items and experiences deemed routine, commonplace, "just the basics." Quality, craftsmanship, and customer care are not top priorities for trading-down purchases. What matters is convenience and, most importantly, rock-bottom prices.

Thanks to the strides of the discount giants and the internet, consumers across all strata have now been given *permission* to spend less. On any given day, in any given Target parking lot, you'll find a Tesla next to a Toyota Civic or a Mercedes next to a minivan. No matter what your zip code, there's probably an Amazon Prime truck rolling through your neighborhood right now.

With this newfound savings, consumers also earn the freedom to trade up for what really matters.

Consider these walking spending contradictions...

- *the starving artist who buys refurbished cameras (trading down) but answers email on her state-of-the-art MacBook Pro (trading up)*

- *the mom who loves the savings of cloth diapers (trading down) but only buys her groceries at Whole Paycheck, er...Whole Foods (trading up).*

- *the business owner who gets her hair done at Supercuts (trading down) but pays $30,000 a year to belong to an exclusive mastermind (trading up).*

More and more buyers are telling us: Sell me my story!

Our trading-up purchases proclaim to the world:

This is what matters to me.

This defines me.
This is who I am and what's important in my life.

The MacBook takes on greater meaning than just a device to type and send. It tells the artist: *I am an innovator.* The grocery shopping trip to Whole Foods doesn't just put food on the table. It affirms for mom that she's doing a good job looking out for her family and caring for the earth her children will one day inherit. The pricey mastermind proves that the business owner is capable of greatness and belongs with top achievers. And the closet promises to show me every morning that I am worthy of a beautiful start.

Disposable income will flow where it matters to the buyer.

With the new trading up, trading down economy serving opposite ends of the spectrum, where does this leave the middle market?

The short answer: obsolete.

The Retail Renaissance

The buying trends that we've highlighted from decades past have only accelerated. As of this writing, Walmart is now by far the world's largest retailer. All signs indicate that Amazon will likely pass them soon. And poor, once-dominant Sears? They never adapted to the changing landscape and are now out of business. Here's a sampling of just a few mid-market brands that have joined them in bankruptcy over the last several years:

Aeropostale, Aerosoles, Aldo, American Apparel, Ann Taylor, Avenue, BCBG Max Azria, Brookstone, Cache, Charlotte Russe, Charming Charlie, Claire's, David's Bridal, Diesel, Forever 21,

OUR TRADING-UP PURCHASES PROCLAIM TO THE WORLD: THIS IS WHAT MATTERS TO ME. THIS DEFINES ME.

Gymboree, J. Crew, JCPenney, Jos. A Bank, Joyce Leslie, Lane Bryant, The Limited, Lord & Taylor, Lucky Brand, Men's Wearhouse, Nine West, Pacific Sun, Papaya, Papyrus, Pier 1 Imports, Quiksilver, RadioShack, Rockport, Rue21, Sports Authority, Things Remembered, Toys "R" Us, True Religion, Wet Seal.

It's a Retail Apocalypse, am I right?

These famous mid-market brands we've known and loved for years are grabbing headlines with their high-profile failures. As stores shut their doors for good, it's easy to get nostalgic. Mournful, even. Our favorite childhood malls are now depressing ghost towns! All this might lead an emerging entrepreneur to wonder: *Is business as we know it doomed?*

You know what they say in the news business: If it bleeds, it leads. What's happening in retail is a sensational shakeup to be sure! But is there anything positive resulting from this upheaval?

In a landmark report released in 2018, industry-leading consulting firm Deloitte presented a study called "The Great Retail Bifurcation." Check this out: Between the years 2013 and 2018, premium retailers—what we've been calling luxury brands—saw their revenues soar by 81%. Over that same span, discount (or value) retailers also gained. They enjoyed a 37% revenue increase. But mid-marketers? They fell flat.

What Deloitte was referring to as "bifurcation" was the widening of the gap between the value and luxury lanes. As the choices became more distinct, consumers more easily found their way onto the lane that mattered most to them for the purchase at hand. The mid-market had lost all appeal.

Our three-lane highway had been reduced to two.

Deloitte's conclusion: We are not in the midst of a retail *apocalypse* but rather a retail *renaissance*. Businesses willing to embrace this change have the potential to thrive. Brands that fail to understand the current trends and remain trapped in the past will fade away. Have you noticed that dollar stores are popping up like mushrooms these days? Meanwhile, upscale malls coast to coast—like King of Prussia in Pennsylvania, Aventura Mall in South Florida, and South Coast Plaza in California—are running at maximum capacity and seeing expansive growth. No apocalypse for them.

"But hang on," you say. "I don't sell goods. Where do things stand with service-based industries?"

The story is the same there, too!

Look at restaurants. Fast-casual chains (read: value!) like Panera Bread and Blaze Pizza are going gangbusters. Upscale is on the rise, too. Capital Grille and Ruth's Chris are having banner years. The mid-market, however, is getting crushed. There is no one left clamoring for the mid-quality, mid-service, and mid-price-points of Applebee's and Outback. People either want a quick bite at reasonable prices or they want to savor the experience and make a memorable night of it. There is no in-between.

The Saddest Stretch of Highway

So where is your place in all this? Which path forward will bring your business success? With the mid-market now off your list of options, should you give it a go selling value? Or luxury?

I've been down both of these lanes. And I know what it's like to choose wrong.

Few people know that before the six-figure smash success of Megan DiPiero Photography, there was a brand I launched called In the Moment Images. Back in 2009, I was what we in the biz call an MWAC—mom with a camera. Photographing families was my jam! I showed up at every playdate and every birthday party armed with my trusty Nikon, ready for action. I posted new albums to Flickr and Facebook, and friends saw real promise. They planted the seed: "Megan, you should do this professionally!" And I've gotta admit, the idea was exciting!

At that time, our family was still reeling from the Great Recession. The unstable market had forced Aric's brand-new mortgage company to collapse, landing us in rough waters with bankruptcy and foreclosure. Like a lot of moms I knew, I was looking for ways to add income to support our family and hopefully still allow me to keep my role as a homeschooling, stay-at-home mom. The timing was ripe for my new business to bloom.

There was just one problem.

I didn't know what the heck I was doing.

Everything was learned on the job. My technique grew from shoot to shoot. Late-night online learn-fests went down every evening after the kids fell asleep. I assigned myself daily art projects to up my skills and connect with other pros. I was working so hard on my craft that it never occurred to me to look at business education.

So how did I price and sell? I let my gut be my guide.

It just *felt right* to price at $250 per shoot.

My circle of mom friends and I were all broke. A couple hundred bucks a pop? That was an amount we could get behind. Sure enough, clients lined up and paid me gladly. I was in business!

Does any of this sound familiar? So many of us start our careers because we have a talent and a passion that gets noticed. I love seeing people follow their dreams and go all-in! What I don't love is the unfortunate death toll that awaits new businesses that fail to plan properly.

What I didn't know back then was that I had unwittingly priced myself in the value lane. Remember: For value businesses to flourish, they must combine low prices with high volume and minimal customer service. But I had the equation all wrong.

When it came to customer service, I was over-the-top devoted! I loved my clients like I loved my own family. I lavished time upon them. From late night what-to-wear phone calls to customized location scouting to handwritten thank-you cards and hand-re-touched, hand-delivered digital images, I was the entrepreneur who served selflessly.

Not surprisingly, all that commitment and connection meant I also messed up the second important component. I completely missed the mark on high volume. Had I been doing a shoot a day, I might have stood a chance of squeaking out a profit, but instead I was spending an entire week per client. Dropping my dollars per hour to below minimum wage.

Between caring for my kids and clients, and with the endless list of learning tasks and challenges, I was really starting to feel burned out. My earnings evaporated as I re-invested over and over into my business. I felt like I was in a money and time pit. I was in way over my head. To make matters worse, despite all the work I was putting in, clients seemed ungrateful and demanding. I found myself up most nights past one a.m. just trying to get in that last round of edit requests and make my clients happy. I was broke, exhausted, and heading for a breakdown.

I needed something big to finally shake me from my sleepwalk.

And then it happened.

A half-hour into my forty-five-minute drive to the beach for a sunset family session, the skies ahead started to darken. Cars to my left and right flicked on their headlights. *Oh no, no. This can't be happening.* You never want to be headed to a shoot and forced to use your headlights. It doesn't bode well. A big, fat splat of rain smacked onto my windshield. As soon as I reached for my wipers,

I SAID GOODBYE TO THE VALUE LANE AND COMMITTED TO LUXURY. BEST DECISION EVER!

my phone started to buzz. The caller ID confirmed my worst fear—it was my client calling.

"Ummm, Megan...are you seeing this? The weather doesn't look so good. Should we reschedule?"

Just then the skies opened up and the downpour began.

My heart sank into a puddle.

Of course I had to reschedule. I had no choice. I told my client I'd call her when we were back home at our calendars and we'd find a new time.

And then I pulled off the road and started to cry.

See, it might have been one thing if all I was losing was money. That was bad enough. This was my only shoot on the books for the week and now instead of dollars on the hour, I was making a big, fat goose egg. Correction: I was making *negative* dollars. Adding insult to injury, my fuel light went on and I realized this hour-and-a-half round trip to the beach was costing me gas money...money I didn't have in my wallet. What really made this cancellation heartbreaking was that I was missing out on an important family moment. This was the night my son was to perform in his first play. He had invited his friends, his daddy, and his Cita and Pop-Pop. My sweet boy hoped mommy could be there, too. But I had agreed to serve my client instead. I was so quick to say yes to making memories for my client and her family that I said no to my own.

I paid for gas with the quarters I could dig up from my console and headed home thoroughly defeated.

That day changed everything. I realized then and there that I owed it to myself, to my family, and yes, even to my clients, to make a significant change. I was no longer willing to move forward without a proper plan. I had a choice...quit now or double down and figure out how to run my business the right way.

It was time to trade up again. We decided to go all-in on education. Several workshops later and $5,000 deeper in credit card debt, I had the information I needed. It wasn't easy...it was terrifying in fact...but I put out a new price list that would assure me $2,500 sales—not $250. I literally 10X'd my prices overnight and rebranded as Megan DiPiero Photography. I said goodbye to the value lane and committed to luxury. Best decision ever!

Roadmap to Success

Okay, we've discussed the way the economy used to work and the way it works now. So, tell me...how did that red pill go down?

Armed with this updated, modern vision of the retail world, it's now easy for us to navigate to the business and life of our dreams. The road ahead is brightly illuminated. Let's recap and reveal the secrets of today's economy.

SECRET ONE: THE MID-MARKET IS DEAD.

Run, don't walk from the mid-market. That place is a graveyard.

The societal pressure forcing buyers into one of three rigid spending lanes has long since been lifted. We now pass, weave, and merge at will. Three lanes have become two. When purchases hold little meaning for us, we trade down to the value lane. There, convenience and rock-bottom prices reign. When we crave aspirational purchases—goods and services that help us tell our story— we trade up for smooth cruising in the luxury lane. The Retail Renaissance is here!

IF CLIENTS BALK AT YOUR PRICES, RAISE THEM.

Secret Two: Small businesses like ours can't succeed in the value lane.

Low price point, high volume, and minimal customer service—this is a challenging equation even for the biggest retailers on the planet. They are constantly using their resources and infrastructure to perfect their process and deliver more convenience at lower prices.

As a small business owner or solopreneur, you can't play effectively at this game. Nor would you want to.

Ask yourself: Did you get into this line of work because you like being an anonymous machine—spitting out transactions en masse and shoving people through an assembly line? Or did you open up shop because you genuinely love people? Because *caring for clients* is your calling?

I have a hunch about people like you who pick up books about empathy. You didn't come to build a factory. You came to build a family. You want to serve trading-up clients who truly value what you do, not trading-down clients who merely treat you like a commodity.

Secret Three: Luxury works in every market.

This one you may not be convinced of yet but hang with me.

I've already told you that my own market of Fort Myers, Florida, is nothing to brag about. The local household income hovers around $40,000, well below the national average. Just like in your market, we have seasonal ebbs and flows. Yet here, as a portrait photographer, I now maintain a year-round sales average exceeding $5,000 per client.

YOU DIDN'T
COME TO
BUILD A
FACTORY.
YOU CAME TO
BUILD A
FAMILY.

EVERYWHERE
WE LOOKED,
"**NOT** IN MY
MARKET"
WAS
BECOMING
#YESINMYMARKET.

Once I realized I'd cracked the code, I started to teach others, too. The first and most common objection my students would always raise was this: "Megan, it's great you have access to clients willing to pay those rates, but that would never work in my market. The people here just don't value photography in that way!"

I heard it from Canadians. I heard it from folks in the Midwest. From folks who live in rural towns in the South. You would not believe how often I've heard this objection raised from folks in Manhattan. London. Even *Beverly Hills!*

"Not in my market." "Not in my market."

Okay, I decided, it's time to retire this money block once and for all.

In 2018, I launched a concept called the $10k Club. My plan was to challenge my mentor students to reach the inspiring goal of selling $10,000 *or more* in a single order. Each new success would be another pin on the map showing our community what's possible. And to sweeten the deal, no matter where the victorious student lived, I would hop a plane to their city and take them out for a celebration dinner. Game on!

Imagine everyone's surprise when the very first pro to join the club was a photographer living in rural Texas. Her studio, like mine, was way off the beaten path. The longhorn cattle population in her one-stoplight town seemed to outnumber the people. I was extra-delighted to learn that she'd met her $10k client in a local feed store. That's networking!

And the success didn't stop there.

The club quickly grew, at first welcoming members from the more populous states such as Florida, New York, and California, but then we had our first international entry: Canada! Never again would I have to hear, "Canadians just won't pay a lot for photography. They don't value it," without having a counterexample to show.

The hits kept coming, and eventually we started running out of regions that didn't have a $10k Clubber. The Midwest? We now have members in Iowa, Wisconsin, and Indiana. The South? Georgia, Tennessee, Arkansas, and Mississippi are all on the board. Out West? Nevada, South Dakota, and Washington registered wins. The Northeast came to play. Jersey, represent! Connecticut, Massachusetts, and Pennsylvania, too. And yes, we finally even cracked London. Plus, for good measure: the Netherlands, Germany, and Australia. Everywhere we looked, "not in my market" was becoming #yesinmymarket.

In big cities and small, in the country and in urban areas, from the Rust Belt to the Sun Belt to the Bible Belt—there are aspirational buyers everywhere! Sometimes you have to drive thirty or sixty minutes to find them—they may not live right in your backyard—but I've yet to find a student who lives in a complete luxury desert.

And remember, we're just talking about photos here! We live in an age when everyone has a pretty darn good camera in their back pocket at all times. If people will pay big for this trading-up service, even when value options abound, it stands to reason they'll pay big for the service you're providing, too.

Are you beginning to believe?

4| EVOLVE BEYOND EXPECTED

Welcome to the luxury lane, my friends! As business owners, service providers, and sales professionals, we now have the awesome opportunity to thrill and delight our clients. We accept the privilege of selling them their stories and we will earn trading-up dollars by delivering on their dreams.

You don't need to be a mega-brand like Bentley, Tiffany, or Gulfstream to command the big bucks. Small businesses can create a huge impact, and with much better margins, too! You just need to put aside the basic and evolve beyond the expected. Remember, you're not just selling "the thing." You're selling a custom solution to your deserving client. If you only delivered on the presenting problem, you'd be missing the mark for sure!

It doesn't matter the industry—from personal stylist to private chef, from custom homebuilder to high-end Realtor, from salon owner to CPA—there is a LUXE business calling your name. All those professions and so many more can bring more satisfaction to their clients and more profits into their bank accounts when they follow the blueprint below. To make it easier to remember, just think of it as an acronym.

LUXE Your Business

L earn the deeper concerns
U p your game
e **X** pand your role
E levate your prices

Four steps to transform your business and start making money that matters. Let's break them down and see how they can be put to work for you.

Learn the Deeper Concerns

My inquiries all sound the same: "Can you take my picture?" I don't let the simplicity of the presenting problem fool me. There is always something deeper. I show my clients I understand them by moving beyond the basics and getting to the heart of their story. *What is the need beneath the need?*

Want a cheat sheet? Check out Maslow's hierarchy.

Trading-up clients, whether they know it or not, are motivated by the top rungs of this pyramid. Your LUXE business has a responsibility to draw them out and identify their true desires.

What do your clients need? Is it **love and belonging?** Take note of the ways in which you can celebrate the relationships and connections that matter to them. Do they need a boost of **esteem**? Everyone wants to feel important. You make that magic happen when you care for your clients—when you notice them, listen, and serve. Also, the very purchase of your services conveys prestige— that feeling of "I've arrived! I deserve this." At the highest level of the pyramid, you may even help clients feel they've reached **self-actualization**. How amazing to use your gifts to help others reach their calling and achieve their potential!

Looking back at that basic question, "Can you take my picture?" Well, yes, I can...and provide so much more!

Up Your Game

Now that you recognize the deeper problems your business will be addressing, it's time to get creative with solutions. Up your game means going above and beyond business as usual. It's all the steps—before, during, and after delivery—that make the impact.

In short, do what others don't.

Quick example from my world: Most photographers think their job starts and stops at image creation. Not me. Making the art is squarely in the *middle* of our complete process. On the front end, we have an in-home consultation to plan and prep. On the back end, I wouldn't dare let those images get relegated to the digital junk drawer. No way. I design custom-framed wall art arrangements to complement their decor. I even install the portraits on my clients' walls and back them with a lifetime warranty.

Do these added steps mean extra time and energy? Of course! But they also create a much higher value for my clients. LUXE service means going the extra mile.

eXpand Your Role

One of the hallmarks of a great service provider is that they never miss an opportunity to make life easier. Expanding your role means to add on related services so your clients don't have to look anywhere else. Your goal is to always anticipate your clients' needs, take away their homework, and offer them a complete and seamless solution.

A personal shopper might incorporate a seamstress to make sure outfits fit as great as they look. A photographer might add a makeup artist to increase camera confidence. A landscaping service could go beyond cutting grass and shaping hedges to offer regular mulching, tree trimming, and seasonal plantings.

What related services could you bundle into your own business to add value and reduce stress and hassle for your clients?

Elevate Your Prices

The work we're describing to LUXE your business will take extra time, attention, and resources. Therefore, it follows suit that prices must increase as well. With higher price follows higher perceived value. So don't be shy here. Make sure you get your prices well into the luxury buying lane so that your client has clarity that you are creating something exceptional.

Meet Piero Pups

Let's put this blueprint to the test. I'm going to stretch my imagination and randomly pick a business that bears no resemblance to my portrait studio. What if I were to design, say, a dog boarding company? How would a LUXE version of this service differ from a traditional kennel? What would it feel like to be a customer? What deeper problems would the brand solve? Let's find out together with a look at my new fictitious business, Piero Pups.

Mr. and Mrs. Miller just put the finishing touches on the big plans for their dream vacation. They'll be spending seven sunny days in the Caribbean, making memories together with their two young kids. They know this is going to be the most incredible trip. But there's just one problem...

What will they do with Winston?

Could their four-legged friend travel along? The fluffy Alaskan malamute wasn't built for warm beaches. Mr. Miller quickly rules out boarding him with Nan and Pops. At nearly ninety pounds, dear Winston can be an affectionate handful. Mrs. Miller suggested a kennel but the moment the words were out of her mouth, she cringed. The kids could barely stand the thought of a week without Winston as it was! The mental picture of sweet Winny trapped indoors and relegated to a cage while they're out building sandcastles would really put a cloud on the family fun ahead.

On the face of things, their problem is simple: Winston needs a place to hole up for a week. But the moment we look beneath the surface, we immediately notice there's more to this story.

Learn the Deeper Concerns

A LUXE business knows all that is at stake. Mrs. Miller craves a reprieve from mom-guilt. Missing their dear companion, the kids will need a salve for the homesick heart—an ability to connect and make sure Winston's doing well. Mr. Miller wants to make sure man's best friend returns in equal or better condition than when they left him. Having raised Winston since his dorm-room days, he wouldn't consider abandoning his buddy.

Without knowing it, the whole Miller family is singing the trading up rally cry: Sell me my story! The Millers don't see Winston as just a pet. They treat him as a beloved member of the family, and he deserves an experience as enriching and enjoyable as the one they're about to embark upon. Luckily, Piero Pups knows what business they're in! No, not the pet boarding biz—the problem-solving biz. Using empathy, they've already considered all these fears and concerns and created solutions to evolve beyond the expected.

Let's put this to work. Complete the exercise below for your business.

LEARN THE DEEPER CONCERNS

Presenting problem:

e.g. Piero Pups dog boarding

What is the need beneath the need?

Piero Pups: love and belonging; salve for the homesick heart; reprieve from mom-guilt

"Sell me my story": What core beliefs define your client?

Piero Pups: the Millers' core belief is "We treat our pet like a member of the family."

Up Your Game

Piero Pups knows they can do better than a basic online booking.

Their "clients for life" mission starts from the very first connection. Every email inquiry gets a prompt and friendly "Welcome to the

Family!" call back. They even offer in-home consultations at the client's convenience to really get to know their guests better and help them find the custom solutions that are right for their needs.

Team member Brittany arrives at the Millers' right on time. Dressed in clean, pressed navy scrubs with the signature Piero Pups smiling dog logo, she is eager to meet her new pal Winston and his loving family. First to answer the bell? Wagging Winston, of course! He is followed by two excited and curious kids, Marcus and Miranda. Brittany crouches down to shake little hands and a furry paw.

This is a listening session as much as a sales session. Brittany interviews the family to learn more about Winston's eating and sleeping schedules, dietary preferences, favorite squeak toys, and terms of endearment. She makes sure to take the kids' feedback very seriously and coaxes them to tell her all about their love for Winny and their hopes for the big upcoming vacation.

Only once Brittany's sure that she has gathered all the necessary feedback does she present her vision: Piero Pups won't just be boarding Winston...they'll be treating him to a vacation experience all his own! During the day he'll enjoy supervised play on their three-acre shaded campus. Brittany has done her homework. She knows the personality of malamutes well and when she mentions how Winston will probably want to be the leader of the pack, Mr. Miller chimes in, "That's our Winny, alright!" She catches the kids' eyes and lights up talking about how Winston will love his evening storytime and snuggles. Mrs. Miller, meanwhile, flips through the VIP luxury suite lookbook and has already picked out a contemporary farmhouse chic designer room. "He'll feel right at home here," she beams.

And what's this? Brittany pulls from her bag a picture book the kids have never seen before.

"Mom! That looks like Winston!"

"It does!" says Brittany. "This is one of my favorites from our storytime library. He's a malamute just like Winston but this guy's name is Harry. Marcus, can I give this to you to read to Miranda on the plane? Oh, and Miranda, do you like coloring books? I have some Paw Patrol in here! In a minute, I'm going to go over some things with mom and dad for Winny's stay. But before I do, I want to tell you the best part about letting Winston be our guest!"

Astutely, Brittany picked up that the family's number one concern was fear of being homesick and missing their pal.

"We would love to send you guys daily photo updates of Winston's vacation. Miranda and Marcus, I know you all are going to have the time of your lives at the beach, but if you ever get homesick, know that Winny is just a call away. Our connection concierge loves to send and receive picture and video updates. How does that all sound to you?"

Winston hasn't even begun his stay and already the Millers know this reassurance has been worth every penny. The Piero Pups campus is impressive indeed, but what made the biggest impact? The way that Brittany listened! Her attention to solving her clients' problems made all the difference and earned their trust.

Would you believe there's still more in store? The week after the Millers return home, Brittany will send them a surprise souvenir photo album showing off Winston's adventures. It's little touches like this that make the Millers raving fans and ensure their repeat business.

UP YOUR GAME

How will you go the extra mile to serve? What will you do that others won't? What parts of your process bring extra value?

Piero Pups: personalized onboarding; in-home family interview; designer luxury suites; 3-acre campus; "storytime and snuggles"; daily text and video updates; souvenir album

eXpand Your Role

The kids run off to color and Brittany's presentation continues.

An on-staff chef will craft a variety of meal options and report back on which ones were Winny's favorites. For their personal peace of mind, Brittany assures Mr. and Mrs. Miller that Piero Pups has 24/7 preferred access to the local vet specialists. They'll make sure Winston is in perfect health throughout. Mr. Miller will be happy to hear that grooming is included—a task he's had on his honey-do list for quite some time. Just as he had hoped, Winston will return to them in even better condition than when they drop him off. And speaking of drop-offs...because the Millers have opted for a weeklong stay, they also qualify for complimentary valet transportation to and from the resort. Piero Pups recognizes that the family will have enough to do getting ready for their flight and don't need the additional homework of driving Winny around. That's one less to-do on their prep list and one more value point for Piero Pups.

Brittany lets the Millers know that all of these specialty services and more are available to them year-round. They won't ever need to look for another pet care resource again. She promises to follow up once they return from their trip with a suggested timeline for future visits. All her furry malamute clients love their monthly groomings!

EXPAND YOUR ROLE

How can you make your client's life easier? What bundled services will help you create a complete and seamless solution?

Piero Pups: on-site veterinarian, nutritionist, groomer; valet transportation

---

Elevate Your Prices

At this point it's quite clear to Mr. and Mrs. Miller that Piero Pups is head and shoulders above the pack. And their prices—considerably higher than other local boarding options—are quite extraordinary too. Knowing that this is everything the Millers have asked for and more, Brittany confidently presents the total. How could they pass on this opportunity and consider anything but the best for dear Winny? Of course they say yes!

⒠LEVATE YOUR PRICES

With higher service comes higher prices. How will you price?

*Complete the **Know Your Numbers** exercise below then return here to record your results.*

MY AVERAGE CLIENT WILL INVEST | $

Clients like the Millers are waiting for you. They would be happy to pay exceptional prices for exceptional service. By following the LUXE model above, you can design an empathetic, aspirational business that will address the deeper needs of your clients and turn them into passionate evangelists. There's only one more big question to be answered: How much should you charge? To figure that out, you'll need to do a little research and reflection.

Know Your Numbers

My favorite TV program for business education—hands down—is CNBC's *The Profit*. Each week, it follows host and serial entrepreneur Marcus Lemonis as he visits a struggling small business and helps the owners figure out where it all went wrong and what steps are needed to turn their company around. The most frequent problem he identifies? These entrepreneurs simply don't know their numbers! They don't really know what their products or services cost and what they need to charge to be profitable. They set their prices by "going with their gut"—not by creating a business plan. Then, when they start seeing red ink month after month, they figure the only solution is to ramp up their marketing and increase their volume. Or, worse yet, they try to expand their way out of trouble and open a new location before fixing the first one. Week after week, Marcus listens to tearful tales of years wasted and debt accumulated as these well-meaning entrepreneurs pour everything they've got into a fundamentally flawed business model.

In my own work mentoring entrepreneurs, I've noticed this trend, too. People will set their original prices based on what they think their friends might be willing to pay for their product or service—an amount that feels "fair." After all, they don't want to take advantage of anyone! They barely consider the costs involved and they don't think at all about their own profits. They figure they'll just keep whatever is left, and hopefully it will come close to making ends meet. Spoiler alert: it doesn't. Before long, they realize they need to raise their prices. But since they're still feeling timid and guilty, they only inch things up marginally—not enough to make a difference. Clients become irritated. The business owner feels lost and demoralized. After struggling for years, they finally reach out to me to try to turn their ship around. At that time, I usually break the hard news that they need to reboot the whole operation.

I'd like to save you that pain. So right now, I'm going to guide you through my four-step process to set your pricing with the end in mind. And it begins with this fundamental question:

How much money do you want to make?

STEP ONE: YOUR INCOME GOAL

Earning a good income is the reason you got into business in the first place, right? So, let's put a number on what it means to be a pro. You are going to put your heart and soul into this. Not to mention startup capital and lots of launch hours to get things rolling. Will it be hard at first? It will! If it were easy, everyone would do it. Success is not guaranteed.

You've got to leave your salaried mentality behind and think differently. Salaried workers clock out at the bell. Business owners have their head in the game round the clock and tie their identity to their calling. As a business owner, you will be doing a lot more work and taking a lot more risk than the average Jane. You owe it to yourself to dream big.

With all this in mind, ask yourself, "What do I want my annual income to be? What will my business make for me?" To make it easier, I want you to think about your income goal three years from now. Why three years, you ask? Because seeing ahead only one year from now is too close to home. Your insecurities will kick in and you'll limit your imagination. Five years out creates the opposite problem. You'll picture a fantasy that feels too make-believe to be real. Three years is just right.

So, three years from now...

...when you're the awesome entrepreneur you always dreamed of

...when you have clients that love you and sing your praises

...when your books are full and your phone is ringing off the hook

...at *that time,* what is the income you're making?

Picture it in your mind. Now tell me. What did you come up with?

$40,000? Go fish. If your dream is to make $40k, let me point you toward a salaried position. You can work far easier jobs with far better benefits and far less stress and make that kind of money.

Think bigger!

3 years from now *[write year]*	
I will hit my income goal of	$

Okay, now we're focused.

Just this step alone will dramatically improve your clarity.

STEP TWO: CLIENT GOAL

In the LUXE business model, less is more. As I've said before, it's not about building a factory. It's about building a family—a loyal community of devoted clients, willing to pay big for a piece of their story. The next step in your business blueprint is to find out just how many clients are right for your workflow, and to do that you need to understand how much you can comfortably handle. This is a marathon, not a sprint! You won't be doing yourself any favors by setting an unsustainable pace and burning yourself out. When I first sat down and added up all the time I was spending to source, book, and serve each of my custom clients, I discovered the average was *thirty hours*. I was floored!

How did I arrive at those thirty hours anyway? To an outsider, a photo shoot appears to take just minutes. All they see is the tip of the iceberg—the hour or so that we spend shooting. What they don't see (and quite frankly, what even I failed to realize) are all the hours spent behind the scenes. Let me show you how to complete an "hours inventory" to get a real sense of the time you're spending with each client.

Here's what you'll do: Create two columns. On the left, list every task needed to complete an entire client transaction. In the right column, assign a time allotment (minutes/hours needed.) Not sure about the time? Err on the side of generosity. Over the years, I've found I notoriously underestimate task completion time. Sure, an album design might only need a few hours start to finish, but procrastination, project interruptions, and client approval delays can easily turn a two-hour project into four!

Here are some ideas about the types of tasks you should consider...

At the heart of your business, we have activities related to sales and marketing. What hours are needed for client acquisition: social media, web advertising, networking, and more? How about in-home consultations and discovery calls? As we saw with Piero Pups, these extra steps are essential to creating value for your brand, but keep in mind, this work takes time. Record the in-person meeting hours plus drive time. What about client and vendor communication? How many hours do you spend on email, text, and phone? Don't forget clerical work: accounting, bookkeeping, data archiving, and maintaining your CRM (client relationship management) system.

It's a lot to think about, so really take some time with this. Spend a good ten minutes letting the ideas flow. Do not put down your pen until you have a complete list.

Add up all those hours. What did you get?

I need [   ] hours per client

Did your number surprise you as much as mine did?

Based on my total, I decided that I could handle two clients per week. At thirty hours per client, that meant sixty hours total to get it all done. If the hours that you came up with exceed your personal abilities or appetite, I have good news for you—you can delegate! In other words: You don't have to do it all alone. In the lean startup years, you might be game for more work while you master your skills and refine your process. But sooner rather than later, you are going to wish to scale back to a more sensible work week. I solved the problem of overwork and overwhelm by training a photo retoucher. That move allowed me to budget forty hours of my time for the important client work—tasks that impact the quality of the sale—and shift twenty hours of non-essential work onto someone else's plate. Voila: two clients a week!

What did your hours reveal?

How many clients can you (and your team) comfortably serve per week?

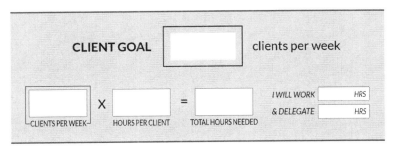

Next, consider how many weeks per year you'll be working. Let's not forget that this business is here to serve you and your chosen lifestyle. How much time do you want off for good behavior?

If you've been grinding it out as an hourly or salaried worker for years, the idea of a few weeks paid break may feel foreign. Remember: You're a business owner now! Set your standards for success. That includes financial freedom and *time* freedom. In my businesses, I have a "work hard, play hard" motto. When it's go time, I'm fully on! But at the end of each quarter, I like to take one to two scheduled weeks off to unplug. These breaks let me travel, spend extra time with my family, relax, refocus, and recharge. You can do the same.

Let's get some of these new goals down.

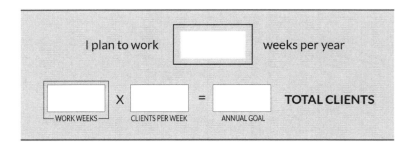

Your picture of success is starting to take shape! We now know what your dream business will deliver for you in terms of income and lifestyle. Cheers to that! We also know how many clients you and your team will comfortably serve. Well, three years from now at least. Remember, our goal here is to plan for your successful business *of the future*. Know that you will build toward your vision over time. There is no need to hire and train an entire team on day one. *Phew!*

STEP THREE: COST OF DOING BUSINESS

We're halfway home here. We just need a little more information and a few more calculations to see where this business is heading. Let's add up your costs. We will break these down into two categories: **fixed** costs and **variable** costs.

Fixed costs consist of all those expenses that exist regardless of how many clients you have. These bills come due whether you're busy or slow. What is the cost to keep this business running? Make sure you have considered what all of your annual costs will be three years from now so that you don't end up in the red.

Here is a short list of fixed costs you'll want to consider during this exercise: rent, utilities, equipment, repairs and maintenance, transportation, software and online subscriptions, office supplies, insurance, accounting, and trade group memberships.

Did you notice what I left off that list? The most commonly forgotten or underbudgeted fixed costs are:

- *Marketing*
- *Education*
- *Helpers*

Marketing. Experts agree that small businesses should allocate 5-15% of their total projected revenue toward marketing. I personally recommend 5%. For small businesses like ours, the most effective outreach is personal and relationship-based. We shouldn't need to spend big, splashy amounts to get attention. Make sure you have the right budget set aside to help you grow. It takes money to make money.

Education. As a high-end service provider, you shouldn't settle for good enough. Always look to improve your skills—that includes your skills as an artist *and* as a business owner. I've consistently spent $5,000 per year on my own education, and I know I'm where I am today because of those growth investments. Attend trade shows, take workshops, hire private mentors, listen to audio books, or all of the above. Do your due diligence to find the coaches that resonate with you and your style. Implement the lessons learned and expect to see a big return on investment.

Helpers. Go back to your hours inventory and highlight the most critical tasks to the success of your business. Selling makes you money. Marketing makes you money. Those are the tasks you will personally take on. Whatever's left ought to eventually be outsourced. Make sure your three-year plan includes a budget line item so that sooner, rather than later, you can delegate work to subcontractors and/or employees, freeing you to focus on what matters. If you're planning on hiring employees, don't forget to budget in payroll taxes. Ask your accountant about this if you have questions.

Got your fixed costs added up? Check!

Now onto **variable costs.** These are expenses that are directly related to each customer you serve. The reason we calculate them separately is that they rise and fall with your volume of clients. Don't have a client? Then you don't have the cost. Fixed costs are defined as a total dollar amount. Variable costs are expressed as a percentage called cost of sales, a.k.a. COS%.

This percentage varies by industry. If you are in a strictly service-based field such as coaching or consulting, you probably have very low variable costs. On the other hand, if you produce and sell a retail product, your COS% could be significantly higher.

Let me give you an example. For me, as a portrait photographer, my variable costs include product costs (albums, prints, wall art, framing, shipping, etc.) and also costs related specifically to services used for the shoot (hair and makeup artists, photo retouching, and catering for full-day sessions.) Whenever I'm unsure if a cost is fixed or variable, I ask myself, "Does this cost only apply when I have a client?" For example, payment processing charges are a variable cost. No client = no cost.

For photography studios like mine, a good target cost of sales percentage is 25%. I know this because our industry has a trade group that periodically surveys successful studios and publishes their findings. Not sure what a good COS% is for you? Look to the experts in your industry for a benchmark. Do some digging. Make sure you're modeling yourself after the high achievers. After all, you are designing a LUXE business here!

When calculating costs, don't underestimate. When in doubt, guess on the high side. We want to make absolutely sure that once this pricing is set, you don't have to increase your rates for a long time. Our goal is to set it and forget it.

Write your costs below.

Annual **FIXED COSTS** for my business	$
My **VARIABLE COSTS** *(cost of sales percentage)*	%

STEP FOUR: PUTTING IT ALL TOGETHER

We are so close now. Hang with me as we cross the finish line. What we'll do next is take your income goal plus all your tallied fixed costs. Divide that by your client goal per year. You now have your total gross profit needed per client.

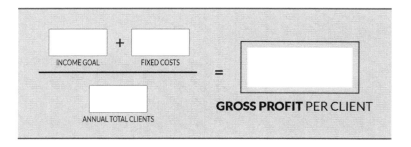

I'll also show you my own numbers from back when I first launched Megan DiPiero Photography so you have a frame of reference:

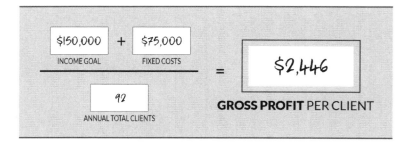

Next let's roll in the variable costs. Take that gross profit needed per client. Divide that by one minus your cost of sales percentage. For example, if your COS% is 25% like mine, then 1 minus 0.25 equals 0.75. Boom! We have your new average sale goal.

The moment we've been waiting for...

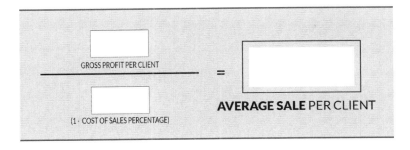

My example:

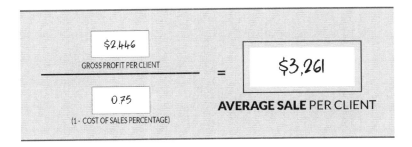

Let's get one more calculation down on paper. Take your average sale goal and multiply that by your annual client goal. This will reveal your annual revenue goal.

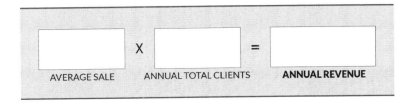

And here is what I came up with...

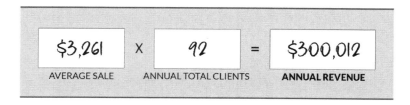

So here we are! Your target average sale and annual revenue goal are staring you in the face. Probably quite a bit higher than you guessed, huh?

When I first ran these numbers, my jaw was on the ground. It instantly became apparent why I had been failing while pricing with my gut. I would need an average sale of $3,261 (not $250!) to build the business and make the income I hoped to achieve. It was quite a wake-up call for me. And I'm sure you're having that same come-to-Jesus moment right now, too.

Let me soften the blow by once again reminding you that, no, you don't have to hit that annual revenue goal this year. And no, you don't have to achieve that client volume right away either. Rome wasn't built in a day. You have three years to ramp up to this success. But what I don't want you to back down from is that average sale goal. Set the correct pricing for your products and services *now* so that you don't have to change it later. Every time you rework your pricing in a substantial way, you'll have to rebuild your client base. I'd rather you start building momentum. Let your client of today be your repeat and referring client for years to come.

Now listen. Despite what I just said, I understand you're going to be tempted to shrink from these big numbers. You're probably feeling insecure and unworthy. If you're anything like me when I first discovered I needed to 10X my prices, you might want to throw up or throw this book into a corner. Don't do either.

Take a few deep breaths. I'm here to help you address all your fears and doubts in the chapter ahead. You got this!

5 | PUSHING THROUGH RESISTANCE

When my kids were little, they were the best of friends. Veda, affectionately called Hooboo, and her big brother, Koan, loved drawing together. That is until Koan started sketching what he called "creepables." He'd make piles of sketches with all the monsters, dinosaurs, and ghoulies that popped into his imagination. For him, it was fun. For Veda, just three years old at the time, it was most troubling. If his art turned up in the living room, Veda would push it off the table. When she found his favorite characters pinned to his wall, she'd squawk and flee the room. Koan's new favorite pastime was driving a wedge in their relationship. After one particularly high-pitched protest, Ko had had enough. He grabbed one of his characters, held it inches from Veda's face, and with total conviction and tough love shouted, "FACE YOUR FEARS, HOOBOO!"

We all found that pretty hilarious, and to our surprise it actually worked!

Veda dug in and accepted the challenge. She faced her fears. Just like that, the worry that was causing her such anxiety and frustration disappeared. She grabbed her own marker to draw, and they were inseparable once more. Now, as teenagers, they laugh and egg each other on to outdo each other with the bizarre. To this day, our little artists love creating absurd, spectacular, and yes, even creepy characters.

It's time for you to face your fears, too. Fear of raising your prices can be overcome by simply shifting your perspective. The first step in the process is understanding where the resistance will come from and the reasons behind it. Once you have this awareness, I'll show you some tactics to alleviate and eventually eliminate your anxiety.

Let's face it: The advice I'm giving you in this book is a little counterintuitive. Very few thought leaders in business are out there saying, "To be successful, make yourself the highest priced option in your market." And because this advice goes against the grain, almost everyone you describe your new business model to will probably want to talk you out of it. After a while, this drumbeat of naysayers might weigh you down and make you second-guess your own plan. I call this phenomenon...

The Conformity Trap

Take a look at these line drawings.

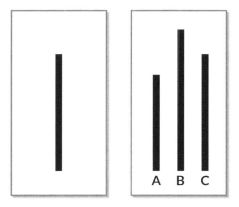

Which line in the box on the right is closest in length to the line on the left? That's easy! Clearly, line C is the match. If I asked fifty people the same question, you would expect they'd all come to the same conclusion, right? Well, that all depends on the conditions under which the question was asked.

In 1951, Solomon Asch decided to determine whether pressure from a group would influence conformity. He invited fifty students from Swathmore College to participate in a "vision test." What followed was actually a psychological study. Each of the unknowing volunteers entered a room with seven other people who were in on the experiment. All eight were then given a series of visual tests similar to the one above and asked to verbally give their answers. The kicker was, the seven insiders had been instructed to occasionally all agree on what was obviously the *wrong* answer and see how often the test subject would feel compelled to go along with the popular response. A number of control groups were also tested with the same questions. Here were the results:

- *When asked individually (no group pressure), subjects answered correctly 99% of the time.*

- *When faced with unanimous agreement from seven strangers, subjects conformed to the wrong answer 33% of the time overall.*

- *75% of the test subjects were convinced to agree on the wrong answer at least once.*

The Asch experiment showed that even on obvious and simple matters, we are influenced by groupthink more than we'd expect. It stands to reason that when faced with much more complex problems (like making business decisions), it might be even more tempting to look to the crowd for guidance.

The thing is, the feedback you'll be getting is going to be the status quo. The conventional wisdom. And yet, statistics show that the majority of small businesses fail. Following the crowd's advice might be like following them off a cliff.

I do have some good news from the Asch experiment. When at least one of the insiders broke ranks and gave the correct answer, the test subjects were much less willing to follow the misguided crowd—only 5-10% of the time, depending on how often the ally answered correctly. The upshot? As long as you have even one successful person telling you that your business plan makes sense, it will be that much easier to shrug off the well-meaning but flawed advice of the majority. Surround yourself with as many successful LUXE business owners as you can, and you can wriggle free from the conformity trap.

Father Knows Best?

Some of the strongest naysaying you encounter will be from those who are closest to you. Family, friends, and industry colleagues will all have their various motivations for talking you into a "safer" pricing model.

For me, my father-in-law was the original no-man. When I first presented my new prices to him, he practically fell off his chair. His reaction was swift and scathing. "No one will pay those prices," he assured me. Worse yet, he added this stinger..."and if they do, they're a sucker."

Punch to the gut.

He wasn't alone in this opinion. My best friend, who was also a photographer, shared a less direct, but equally discouraging message. She cringed when I told her my new prices. "Ooo. I don't know, Megan," she warned. "I think you should re-think that. I'd never pay that for photos. And I don't know anyone else who would either. Trust me. I've been doing this for years."

Here I'd done my business analysis. Worked my numbers. Crafted my plan. And yet those closest to me were telling me I was wrong. And to make matters worse, this wasn't just the Asch line drawing in dispute. We weren't talking about a simple vision test. This felt like a morality test too. My father-in-law as much as called me unethical for overcharging. My friend was making this about personal trust—would I go against her years of experience? Who was I to defy her judgment and counsel? And meanwhile, there were two other crowds still to poll. I hadn't dared to ask my previous clients. My heart was telling me they would all take the price hike as a betrayal. And the internet? Forget about it! In photography forums, my community signaled that it was our moral imperative to charge "reasonable" rates and provide for our friends and neighbors. All the while overlooking that we were failing to provide for own families and running ourselves out of business with unsustainable prices.

What was I to do?

First things first, I had to depersonalize these perceived attacks. If I could take my ego out of things and understand their motivations, I'd have a better chance of dodging the emotional baggage being slung my way.

I've learned over the years that there are three main reasons why other people try to bring us back in line:

- *Protection*
- *Self-Preservation*
- *Propriety*

Protection. The loudest warning sirens were coming from the ones who loved me most. When we step outside the protective confines of the herd, we expose ourselves to danger. Mom, dad, your spouse, and bestie—they just want to keep you safe. Being an entrepreneur is threatening enough, and here we go, doubling down on the unfamiliarity and risk by pursuing this strange niche of LUXE enterprise. Why can't we just settle down and get a nice, predictable, salaried job? When our loved ones push back, it's because they are afraid for us. Remembering that their advice is an act of love may help you appreciate and overcome their concerns.

Self-Preservation. My friend may not have admitted it, but my proposed approach was a challenge to her chosen path. If I found fast success with this higher pricing, that would force her to rethink (and maybe regret) her own strategy of charging less for all those years. The easier and more comfortable course was for her to assume she already had optimal pricing and that I was doomed to fail. As you might expect, this reaction gets stronger in proportion to the time the individual has spent "paying her dues."

Propriety. Our internet communities and social circles each uphold their own internal values. *This is how we do things round here.* There is a code of ethics in each community. My Facebook mom groups (where I found most of my clients in my early days) prided themselves on coupon clipping and swapping deals. These same groups often bred photographers like me who were out to bring in extra cash for the family. The unspoken value implied: good moms save money. Presenting a luxury service (read: high price) in this type of group was almost a betrayal. Mind you, this doesn't mean it's impossible to win folks over. But if we've learned anything about conformity, I stood a better chance presenting my case one-on-one than I did posting in a group forum.

With this understanding in mind, it was much easier for me to turn down the volume on the very loud voices shouting their warning cries. I told myself, they have their perspective and I have mine. Remember how 99% of test subjects could correctly find the right line match when left to their own devices? I knew Line C was the right choice. My head told me to defy the crowd and go with the business model I had put down on paper.

Let me fast forward and tell you what became of those relationships and external crowd pressures. My best friend and I drifted apart. As my success as a luxury photographer grew, we had less in common. And she remained resistant to change. We slowly parted ways and I opened the door to new friendships that bolstered me and spurred me on. The internet groups that would try to limit my aspirations? I quietly left them. In time, I created my own online community of supportive LUXE professionals.

And what about my father-in-law? I realized I was giving his opinion a lot of weight because I respect him. He's a successful lifelong entrepreneur himself, and I really do care about how he perceives me and my business. I wanted to make him proud. But more importantly, I wanted to make me proud, and therefore I needed to follow my own path. After several years of skepticism and doubt, he finally said out loud to me, "Well, looks like you know what you're doing." These measured words spoke volumes. I had won him over!

Too Much Competition

While you're dealing with the fears and doubts thrown your way by friends and family, you'll also be battling anxiety from within. Top among the daunting list of insecurities: "But how will I compete in this crowded market?"

It feels like everyone is doing what you're doing. You just know so many professionals in your industry. It's hard enough to stand out as it is, and now that I'm suggesting you raise your prices, your blood pressure is rising too. Won't pushing up your rates just push people away?

Have no fear. Remember our three spending lanes? Businesses from one lane can completely disregard those in the others. Do you think Ruth's Chris Steak House is concerned when the Arby's down the street runs a 5-for-$10 special on roast beef sandwiches? Heck no! The same customer can eat fast food for lunch twice a week and then drop $300 on a fine dining experience to celebrate her anniversary.

You will only be competing with other LUXE businesses, and there are not as many of those in your industry and market as you think. There are literally hundreds of professional photographers in my city, but probably only four or five who charge as much as I do. And most of my clients are only familiar with one or two of those.

Can that be true, you ask? Quick exercise. Without looking at your phone, call to mind the names of all the luxury interior designers in your area. How about private chefs? Personal stylists? Most people aren't able to name more than one from each category, if any. As long as you're that top-of-mind professional whom others know, trust, and like, they won't be shopping around. Forget about competition.

There are more than enough clients for all of us here at the top.

I Wouldn't Pay That

Another of the internal fears that might be holding you back is this: *I wouldn't pay these prices. How can I ask others to do so?*

We'll talk later about how to find your ideal clients. But for now, I just want you to realize that you don't have to *be* your own ideal client.

When I first started as a luxury portrait photographer, I was living in a starter home in the bad part of town. I didn't drive a fancy car or wear designer clothes. All of my friends were stay-at-home moms, and not the kind who regularly host charity galas. At that time, the thought of spending $3,000 (or $10,000!) on a photography session was alien to me. None of my friends lived like that. It made me feel a little uneasy to set those prices in the first place.

But then I thought about it with a little perspective. The guy selling Ferraris down at the dealership doesn't necessarily *own* a Ferrari. A real estate agent can sell multi-million-dollar listings even if they don't yet live in a mansion themself. And you don't have to be the kind of person who spends lavishly on whatever service it is you provide in order to justify offering those rates to the public.

That's not to say you won't become that person eventually. Over time, I have become my own ideal client. Keep pushing through all those types of resistance you'll inevitably face: external, internal, real and imagined.

Success lies on the other side!

Face Your Fears

They say the fear of public speaking is stronger than the fear of death. Imagine a room with four hundred seats. From backstage, the lights are so bright I can barely make out the silhouette of endless rows of chairs. My audio tech adjusts my mic and I flinch as the cold wire runs down my back. My hands are fidgeting and my heart can't decide if it wants to jump out of my chest or seize up entirely.

Will I forget my script? Will I be the person they expected? Will they laugh along with me...or at me?

It's ten minutes before my big debut speaking performance and the main doors have just opened. It looks like it's gonna be packed. I thought I feared an empty room. Now, I realize a full room is somehow worse. I take a last look at my notes and remember to stash my phone away so I won't have any distractions. Just before powering it down, I spy my friend Lora on caller ID.

YOU DON'T HAVE TO **BE** YOUR IDEAL CLIENT TO **SERVE** YOUR IDEAL CLIENT.

"What's up?" I say frantically. "I'm about to go on."

"I know that," she says gently. "Why do you think I'm calling you? Are you freaking out?"

I don't respond but a deep forced breath tells the tale.

"I suspected as much." Lora gets it. "Listen. Before you get up on that stage, I have a big question for you."

"I'm listening," I reply.

"Okay. Here goes...are you going on that stage because you want self-glorification?" Long pause to let this sink in. "Is this all about your ego and making a name for yourself?"

I laugh good naturedly. "No, of course not."

"Okay then. So, here's my next question. Instead, are you going out there because you have an important message that others need to hear? Are you up there because you have figured out a piece of the puzzle and want to bring it to others to make their lives better?"

"Yes! That one! I'm here today to help!"

"Well, there you go!" I could just picture her smiling. "You have nothing to worry about. You know you are here to serve. Now get out there and make this world a better place today!"

I remember this life-changing phone call every time I have a speaking engagement. And I also conjure it up when I'm about to hit a networking meeting, or dial up a new lead, or head into an ordering appointment—any time self-doubt starts creeping in. I love the concept so much I've made a mantra out of it:

Don't be nervous, lead with service.

See, the problem is, so often in our lives we get caught up in *how will this reflect on me?* Essentially, we're operating from a place of ego.

"Don't be nervous, lead with service" means not making what you're about to do about you but instead looking outward at the person whose life you're about to make better.

If I focus entirely on others and channel all my energy toward service, I simply cannot fail. My intention will be felt. My work will be guided by empathy, commitment, and love. I really have nothing to worry about.

Find Your Motivation

Another way to get out of your own head is to think about who and what your business is supporting. What were you dreaming about when you wrote down your big income goals? Will you be providing for your spouse and children? Creating a better lifestyle for yourself with travel and time to relax? Are you supporting a larger team?

Put that vision at the forefront of your mind. Remember that being a professional, by definition, means making money. You have chosen this career and you are shaping your income because you want to provide a better life for you and yours. If you just wanted to do your craft, free from the worries of a paycheck, you could certainly choose to be a hobbyist. But because you are a pro, you must focus on that income goal.

We make a business that matters by providing service that changes lives. And receiving money that changes lives.

When I first saw my numbers in black and white, I was terrified.

DON'T BE NERVOUS, LEAD WITH SERVICE.

Who was I to ask for such big sales? I questioned my own worth. Extensively. Exhaustively. But you know whose worth I never questioned? I never doubted what my family meant to me. If this was to be our income, if I was to be the breadwinner, I would need to stand up for us.

The very first price list that I ever created was a beautiful hardcover folio. On the back cover, where no one would ever look, I printed a picture of my smiling kids. Every time I grabbed the folio from my travel case, my right hand touched their faces. It worked like magic to fill me with conviction. I could say the scary prices out loud for Veda and Koan and the better life I wanted to build for them.

Rip Off the Band-Aid

A common reaction from people who just completed the pricing exercise goes something like this: "Oh wow...I need to average $3,000 per client? I'm not ready to charge that right now. Let me start by charging $1,500, and I'll work my way up to $3,000 after I have more experience/better equipment/a nicer storefront/etc."

Here's the problem with taking half-measures. Let's say in Year One you fire up your marketing engines and sell your little heart out. You start making new connections. Serving up solutions. And, as expected, hit your (watered down) average sales goal of $1,500.

In Year Two, all your marketing efforts start to bear fruit. Testimonials from happy clients are rolling in. Your phone is ringing with new prospects. There's a buzz about town and you have more bookings than ever. You are nearing your client volume goal. You tell yourself, "I'm ready! In Year Three it's time to raise those rates like I always said I would."

So finally, you make the increase to $3,000. Your existing clients note that your prices have gone up. Not just a little, but double! Many of them walk. That great referral base you just spent years building? They are texting and calling with anger and confusion. "How come I sent my friend your way and she says you're charging her double for the same thing you did for me?" She has a point. The trust they gave you has been broken by this new and sudden price shift. You find yourself in the unfortunate position—once again—of alienating your loyal client base.

Do not attempt the gradual approach. Each price shift will bring new resistance from your existing clients and force you to go back to the marketing drawing board. It will be exhausting for everyone.

Instead, rip off the Band-Aid. Set your prices where they need to be from the start. Then, offer your first few clients a special discount on those prices. This will allow you to increase your confidence while still setting the correct expectations for future business. It will also be your opportunity to generate positive buzz and evangelists. Everyone loves a deal, and you want these early adopters to be blown away by your experience.

Here's a sample script:

I am so excited to introduce my new service! Tell you what... if you would like to be one of my portfolio clients, I would love to offer you early access with a $500 credit to get you started. Select whatever you love most with that credit and if you're tempted to buy more, you'll have access to my complete product line. I'm only making this available for my first three clients and I'd love it if you would be one of them. Want to talk *more about it?*

What makes this approach so effective?

You've softened the impact of saying that big, scary number. You've shown wonderful generosity with the $500 credit and your client feels like an honored insider. In my experience, she'll almost always end up buying more than what the voucher covers. In the process, you've also introduced her to your real and true pricing— opening the door to future repeat and referral business.

You know what else? It won't take you long to work up the courage to charge full price. My plan when I started was to offer these discounts to my first ten clients. To my surprise, the first two I worked with didn't blink at the final invoice and gladly paid thousands! The fear had all been on my end. Going forward, I was comfortable taking the training wheels off and decided to drop the voucher. I started saying my full prices with confidence and never looked back. Now I hear this all the time: "Megan is expensive. *But she's worth it!*"

60% Fabulous

An eye-opening internal report by Hewlett Packard once found that men will apply for a job when they meet 60% of the qualifications, but women only if they meet 100%. And get this—the men get the job!

Once I learned this, I immediately shifted my worldview. It helped me understand that I don't have to be perfect to be effective. I now raise my hand when I see an opportunity. I take a step forward before my name is called. I give myself permission to advance and create the life and career I want.

Maybe you're not feeling 100% qualified today. And that's perfectly okay. If you're willing to admit, "You know what? I'm not perfect. But I'm 60% fabulous!" then you are ready to step forward and stake your claim too.

Now let's go find those clients!

6 | SHE ~~MARKETS~~ MAKES FRIENDS

How many postcards did you take out of your mailbox and pitch directly into the trash this week? How many newsletters hit your inbox and made you click unsubscribe? It's been estimated that the average person is bombarded with anywhere from 4,000 to 10,000 ads per day. *Per day!* Billboards, robocalls, magazine spreads, sponsored posts, TV, radio, and YouTube spots all competing for our attention. Unfortunately for the marketers pushing these messages, very few of their attempts manage to register, much less engage.

The rule of seven states that consumers need to see an ad at least seven times before the message even gets *noticed*. If the biggest companies in the world and in our community are battling for attention, what can we do to stand out from the crowd? Solopreneurs and small businesses like ours have limited resources, so we can't waste our time and money on inefficient marketing tactics.

The good news is that you and I have a secret weapon that helps us cut through the noise. Using our empathy advantage, we can tune in to the needs of the people around us and offer up solutions that will make their lives better. In this chapter, I'll show you how to connect directly, one-on-one with the people who need what you have to offer. While others are pushing their message out, I'll show you how to draw people in.

Coffee Is for Connectors

You may have heard the old sales adage "Always Be Closing."

In one of the greatest movie monologues of all time, Alec Baldwin steals the scene as he lectures a team of underperforming real estate salesman in *Glengarry Glen Ross*. Sent down by Mitch and Murray from the head office "on a mission of mercy," this slick-haired shark doesn't mince words. He lays down the hammer and informs the team of this month's sales contest: "First prize is a Cadillac Eldorado. Second prize is a set of steak knives. Third prize is you're fired."

The haranguing continues, "...only one thing counts in this life! Get them to sign on the line which is dotted! ...A-B-C. A—always, B—be, C—closing." You close or you hit the bricks, pal.

While scenes like these make for great cinema and unmatched quotability[2], they also shine a spotlight on everything we fear about sales. It looks like a world populated by greedy con men, willing to say whatever it takes to get theirs. It's predators versus prey.

---

2 Who can forget Baldwin's character barking across the room at the bedraggled Shelley Levene, played by Jack Lemmon: "Put. That coffee. Down! Coffee's for closers only."

This image of the ruthless salesman runs rampant in our collective conscience. From frontier hucksters touting the wonders of snake oil to Wall Street brokers cold-calling leads to pitch them penny stocks, we see something malicious in aggressive marketing. It's the reason so many of us dread the thought of appearing "too sales-y" in our approach with prospects.

If winning means taking advantage of others, count us out.

Good news...no, great news! It's time to rethink what being a sales professional is all about. We need an updated ABC lesson:

- *A: Always*
- *B: Be*
- *C: Connecting!*

Connecting is at the heart of what I do. By focusing on relationships (clients for life!), my approach stands in stark contrast to the con man and swindler. The Glengarry boys designed a process that was purely transactional. *I win when I take your money.* My goal instead is to create win-wins and bring value to my client. *I've earned your money when I've solved your problem.* We're on the same side.

In my mind, it's all about serving. Marketing and sales are not separate endeavors, but one continuous loop.

Here's what I mean by that...

My goal is to meet strangers and turn them into friends. I look for opportunities to serve my friends and bring value to their lives through what I do. They are then so thrilled with the results that they become evangelists, introducing me to their friends who eventually become clients as well. Meanwhile, my connection never stops with my original contact. She comes back for more, offering repeat business and endless referrals. This cycle is a process I call "Connection Marketing."

In our ever-changing world, marketing trends will come and go, but real human connection never goes out of style. To build your reputation and generate positive word of mouth, aim for long-term, authentic relationships built on a foundation of trust and commitment. The next time you're tempted to say, "I need more clients," just translate that in your mind to, "It's time to make more friends."

Finding Your Ideal Client

The great thing about living in a trading up, trading down world is that we can open our doors to committed consumers from all walks of life. Treat all your clients like gold, I say! I love ringing up sales with an Amex Black card. And I love it even more when clients save up for the opportunity to splurge. It really is a blessing to be able to work with anyone and everyone.

Yes, we want every client who wants us. But we also must be strategic with our outreach. Your goal when marketing is to focus your energies where they will have the greatest impact for your business.

What I'm dancing around here is something you might have already realized...your ideal client might not be you, or your sister, or your current group of friends. *"Aww, man!"* you protest. *"Does this mean I have to work with rich people?"* No, my friend! You get to work with rich people! Be open to all the people around you and continue to stretch beyond your comfort zone and current contacts. Abundance and opportunity lie ahead!

Keeping an open mind, let's start the process of visualizing your ideal client. If your business is brand new, you'll need to rely on your imagination to picture this person. If you've been established for a while, you can instead call to mind your favorite past customers. Reflect on your best spenders and your big-time evangelists. Bonus points for people who are both! Note any key characteristics that repeat among these VIPs.

Now let's create a profile for your ideal client avatar with the following exercise:

Who is this person? Give her a name. Think through the details of her life. What does her typical day look like? Where does she spend her time, talent, and treasure?

What are her aspirations and interests? What values are closest to her heart and how would she like the world to see her? What does she care about and who does she care for?

Finally, what troubles her? What problems is she trying to overcome? What frustrations and insecurities does she wish she could resolve?

Now that you've identified *who* your dream client is, let's consider *where* she's most likely to be found. Your mission as a Connection Marketer is to position yourself where your paths are most likely to cross. Once you've connected with this person, you want to hear her say, "Wow! You are everywhere! You know everyone!" You won't really be everywhere of course. Just everywhere *she* is!

Quick sidebar: What if you don't live and work in an area that contains luxury clients—people with disposable income and the willingness to splurge? What then?

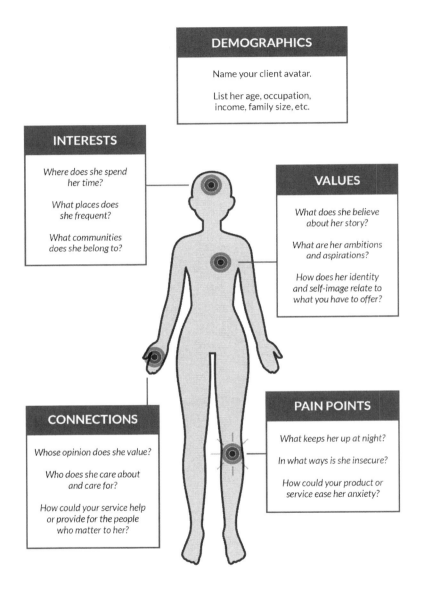

DEMOGRAPHICS

Name your client avatar.

List her age, occupation, income, family size, etc.

INTERESTS

Where does she spend her time?

What places does she frequent?

What communities does she belong to?

VALUES

What does she believe about her story?

What are her ambitions and aspirations?

How does her identity and self-image relate to what you have to offer?

CONNECTIONS

Whose opinion does she value?

Who does she care about and care for?

How could your service help or provide for the people who matter to her?

PAIN POINTS

What keeps her up at night?

In what ways is she insecure?

How could your product or service ease her anxiety?

First up, let me ask you...are you sure about that?

When I first started, I only knew the people and places that were part of my world and my day-to-day activities. My friends and I hung out where we could spend little or no money: public libraries, community parks, and potluck playdates at each other's homes. As my minivan cruised from point A to point B, I missed a whole world just outside my view. Tucked away down sidestreets along my familiar routes were affluent communities I never knew existed. Many of my students in other markets share the same eye-opening experience of finding previously unknown pockets of wealth hiding in plain sight.

If you're truly convinced you live in a luxury desert, don't be afraid to travel. Fully 90% of my customers live forty to ninety minutes away. I never regret the commute. I figure every time I hop in my car, I have the potential to make thousands. Plus, I use all that great drive time to sharpen up my business skills listening to audio books. Multitasking for the win!

Let's brainstorm the places where your ideal client spends her time. Consider these four categories to get the wheels turning:

Businesses. Where does your avatar spend her dollars in the community? What local businesses does she frequent? Try to identify companies with a client base that naturally aligns with your own. I suggest you patronize these businesses, get to know their owners, and be on the lookout for marketing collaboration opportunities.

Not-for-profits. Your client may also be involved with local charities, philanthropic causes, and not-for-profit enterprises. Annual galas and fundraising parties may be a big part of her social calendar. What causes do you imagine your avatar supports? Don't forget to consider churches and private schools in this category. Get involved with these organizations for the chance to have meaningful interactions with your ideal client.

Networking groups. I like these organizations as a way to meet and connect because here you are actually encouraged and expected to talk up your business. You may have already heard about BNI, Rotary, and your local chamber of commerce. There are all kinds of smaller groups—Toastmasters, Optimists International, and American Business Women's Association to name a few. Visit as a guest and commit to regularly attend one or two groups that resonate with you. Many of your ideal clients are probably business owners themselves and trying to make connections too!

Online forums. More and more, our clients can be found socializing on the internet. Lifelong friendships and business connections happen in these virtual networks. Identify which platforms and communities your client is spending time in and join the conversation.

Flipping the Like Switch

There's your dream client, right over there! Now, how will you win her over? People do business with people they know, trust, and like. Essentially, become her friend and you've got your in. Making friends is something many of us take for granted but the mechanics can be taught.

In his book *The Like Switch,* Dr. Jack Schafer explains the "Friendship Formula" for getting anyone to like you. Schafer was a special agent for the FBI's behavioral analysis program, and his high-stakes job was flipping hardened terrorists into allies. (Luckily, our targets won't offer that much resistance!) He simplified his techniques of persuasion into these four building blocks: proximity, frequency, duration, and intensity.

Proximity means putting yourself in contact with people—getting out into the world and being where they are. Studies have shown that face-to-face interactions are much more impactful and memorable than the digital alternative. **Frequency** and **duration** mean that the more contacts you have with that person, and the longer those contacts are, the more inclined they are to like you. And **intensity** measures your ability to bring value to them through your connection.

Making friends boils down to this: show up regularly and make yourself useful.

This formula is why traditional networking groups can be so effective. There's proximity (you're all gathered together in the same room), frequency and duration (regularly scheduled meetings), and intensity (members socialize, talk about what matters to them, and give each other referrals). Any time you can introduce these four elements, you've got a Connection Marketing opportunity. Parent-teacher associations, spin classes, church picnics, even regular monthly salon visits...these are all places where I have cultivated friendships and eventually won over clients.

Beyond the Friendship Formula, what else contributes to likability? As Dale Carnegie wrote in his famous book *How to Win Friends and Influence People,* "You can make more friends in two months by becoming interested in other people than you can in two years by trying to get other people interested in you."

I'll never forget the time I met Rob. I was one month into my business, and things were coming along. My home studio was newly renovated, my portfolio was polished and professional, my makeup artist was on board, and everything was ready to roll. There was just one problem. No clients! I said to myself, *Megan, you know who your ideal client is. And you know where to find her. It's time to get out there and make some friends!* I set off on a mission to connect.

I knew my prospect would care about image—how she presents herself to the world matters. Surely a posh custom clothier in the swanky part of town would be a natural place to cross paths. A quick web and social media search revealed just such a place and in no time at all, I had uncovered the names and pictures of the boutique's owners. The very next day, I made a plan to drive out and introduce myself.

My mission was to act cool, despite all the butterflies in my stomach. I was not there to make a sales pitch, but just to jumpstart a conversation. The moment I entered the store, I recognized Rob. *Thanks, internet!* Rather than march right up to him, I took some time to browse the collections. People like it when you patronize their business. I'd thought ahead and come prepared with a small budget to buy. Rob takes an interest in all his guests and within moments we were chatting. I focused on giving him (and his pride and joy, his hand-selected merchandise) the spotlight. I listened. I learned. And I let the conversation flow.

I was prepared with questions like these:

- *I'm new here. What ways have you found most effective to get plugged in with our community?*

- *Your store is beautiful! How did you pick this location?*

- *How can someone like me help bring you more clients? Who's your perfect match?*

Rob was enamored with me and my line of questions. Since I had deliberately picked the early morning hours when I knew business would be slow, he had time to spare. He was very interested in sharing his expertise. The Dale Carnegie principle was working. People really do love it when folks show an interest in them.

Putting yourself out there can be nerve-racking, but I'd done my homework and pre-planned some questions to ease the fear factor. Plus, the pressure evaporated when I realized I didn't have to talk about myself at all. To the contrary, the less I talked about me, the better! I was a generous conversationalist and estimated I had talked only 40% of the time and listened 60%.

Because I provided value—listening and showing I cared about what mattered to him—Rob was eager to return the favor and extend value to me. He dialed up a friend at his favorite not-for-profit and got me an invite to an exclusive fundraising event happening that very night in the most prestigious neighborhood in town. Of course, I accepted the invitation! Once there, Rob introduced me to the who's who that would form the core of my clientele for years to come. And as he did, he always repeated, "You have to meet Megan. She has the heart of the community." Over and over, "the heart of the community." What gave him that impression? It wasn't what I'd said. It was how I'd *listened*.

The most important thing you can learn in sales and marketing is this: No one cares about you. Okay, let me soften that a bit. Your closest friends and fans will be delighted to see you shine. But those relationships take time to nurture. The new people you are trying to reach don't want to know about the details of your life, the recognition you've earned, or the awards you've won. They want to know this:

What can you do *for me?*

In the words of Theodore Roosevelt, "People don't care how much you know, until they know how much you care." At the beginning of a relationship, let others have the attention. No more, "Look at me!" but rather, "Look at *you!*"

People, Not Things

Early in my career, I learned that I didn't need to carry business cards. They would burn a hole in my pocket at networking meetings, galas, and while out and about town. Print collateral can tend to act as a crutch and lead to bad habits. To quote the late great comedian Mitch Hedberg, when someone hands you a flyer, it's like they're saying, "Here, *you* throw this away."

When I'm out in the community, my goal is to create and nurture deep relationships. If I shove a business card in your hand, we've just closed a curiosity loop. Instead, I want to open the conversation and get to know you better. If we want to keep in touch, I'll put your number right into my phone. I'll text you a friendly message on the spot so we can stay connected. When I really hit it off with someone, I ask if I can friend them on Facebook. The running joke in my family is that I don't have a personal page. I have a business page and a "business page lite." My personal feed has become my networking hub and therefore I always have my game face on. By staying focused on others—commenting, liking, connecting—I can put the Friendship Formula to good use. The next time we are face-to-face (proximity), we'll both have benefited from multiple points of contact (frequency), and I'll have demonstrated I am on her side and a valuable person to know (intensity).

Another marketing tactic I always advise against is the event bag stuffer or "swag bag." People just don't look at collateral they didn't ask for and 99% of it is pitched straight in the trash. A much better use of your marketing budget would be to attend the trade show or event in person and meet people directly. Better yet, get on the event committee and bring value to the organizers. If you think your ideal client will be on the scene, that's where you want to be. Get plugged into those communities.

Serve, Serve, Ask

Can all this really lead to a sale though?

Remember, my mission at the outset of this chapter was to show you how to cut through the noise and put Connection Marketing to work for you. Once you've committed to the relationship approach, things will really start to turn in your favor. While those thousands of ads per day are shouting in our clients' faces, we'll be whispering in their ears. And it's this subtle and gentler approach that works wonders!

I always make it my mission to Serve, Serve, Ask.

First, I provide value.

Then I provide more value.

I may provide still *more* value.

And then, eventually, my opportunity will come. I'll be ready to make the Ask. A common rookie mistake is to march up to someone and ask them for a favor before the relationship's been established. Ever had a brand-new contact ask you to hand out a stack of their business cards? Annoying, right? It's like a stranger walking up to you at a bar and asking you to marry them. Slow down, buddy! If you want folks to do for you, first you need to show you're there for them. We build that trust and reciprocity through serving.

What does an act of service look like? We've already discussed a few. Noticing people. Caring about them. Giving them the spotlight. That all counts. Serving might also mean providing value to their business. I wasn't kidding when I asked Rob, "How can someone like me help bring you more clients?" I am always on the lookout for how I can better connect my friends and business allies. The gift of a referral is tremendously appreciated.

I also look for opportunities to use my tangential skills to benefit my contacts. Photographers like me are experts at assessing light. When a business coach friend of mine launched her new YouTube channel, I noticed. Her message was on point, but I saw how she could improve the scene and get a more flattering look on camera. A fifteen-minute phone call from me provided her with the lighting tips she needed to shine in her next release. Her audience noticed the improvement and she was delighted for my help.

A service act can even be as simple as providing your time and elbow grease to a worthy cause. I craved the chance to get insider access to an elite private school in my area. So many of my clients had children enrolled there that I knew our businesses could benefit each other. When they announced their annual fundraising event, I jumped at the chance to assist. Even after the event had wrapped, I stuck around to help the organizers clean up. That night I rubbed elbows with the headmaster, the social media marketer, the teachers, and many committed parents. A couple hours of moving chairs, breaking down tables, and stashing decorations built a strong foundation of trust. Thanks to the connections made, the next year my business with that school tripled!

Keep interacting with people to provide value and stay top of mind. Serve and serve some more. Then, when the time is right, you'll have earned the chance to ask for their business.

Making a Great Offer

Whether you're extending a personal invitation to that special prospect or running a public promotion for your entire community, here are the four components every great offer has in common:

- *An irresistible deal.*

Your offer should feel like it's right on that line of *almost*, but not quite, too good to be true. It should pain your client to turn it down.

- *Urgency and/or scarcity.*

There needs to either be a time limit on your offer (urgency) or a limited number of spots available (scarcity), or both. It's easy to put off taking action on an open-ended offer. Scarce offers feel exclusive and valuable, and make people feel privileged to have won the opportunity.

- *A call to action.*

People need to be prompted to accept your offer. This can be as simple as the classic, "Call now to book!" but if you're making the offer in person, you have even better options. You could say, "How's Wednesday afternoon for you?" or, "Do you have your calendar handy? Let's pick a time." If you charge an up-front deposit or session fee, you might simply ask, "What credit card do you want to put this on?"

- *Repetition and follow up.*

Remember the rule of seven I mentioned earlier? An offer made just one time is easy to ignore. When you're running a promotion of any kind, expect to need a lot of repetition before you get traction with your audience. Even when extending a personal invitation to an audience of one, don't be afraid to check back in with her. People are busy and it's easy to get sidetracked. She wants to say yes. She just needs you to follow up.

Ready to see how this works in real life? Let me tell you about the million-dollar workshop that almost never happened.

For years, I had taught a live course on the business of photography. This workshop proved nothing short of life-changing for our students. We knew we had something valuable on our hands and were eager to share it with the world. Aric and I decided it was time to hire a professional studio and record the course for sale online.

One of my favorite sayings is, "Rich begins with risk." We took on a whopping five-figure debt (nothing to sneeze at in my early days) to secure the studio and crew. To cover our costs and to create an engaging presentation, we knew we'd need to sell thirty tickets to fill our live audience. So, how would we craft our great offer?

First up: an **irresistible deal.** The recorded course was set to have a price tag of $1,200. Live attendees would get in on a special—only $590. What a deal! We planned the discount to be steep enough to create temptation, but not so extreme that it would call into question the value of the course. We also introduced **scarcity** and **urgency**—only thirty seats available, first come first served, and the filming date was on the calendar. Time was ticking! **Call to action**? Check! We had a landing page at the ready that urged interested folks to Book Now and made the signup process easy.

RICH BEGINS WITH RISK.

Finally, **repetition**. We planned to reveal the big event on three platforms: our website, our Facebook group, and a newsletter.

All systems were go! The launch day arrived, and we held our breath as the offer went live.

Within minutes, we immediately sold the first spot! High fives all around. This was going just as planned! And then a week passed with...nothing. No more inquiries. No more bookings.

I was freaking out.

If we couldn't sell all thirty seats, we'd be underwater. We asked ourselves the hard question: *Should we cancel this thing?* Maybe we had misread the market. Maybe we could still get the deposit back from the film studio and go back to the drawing board. We thought it over and decided that no, we'd come too far. This workshop was happening, and we'd just have to 10X our efforts to fill those seats.

So, I went all-in. I emailed, texted, sent out *more* newsletters, and personally invited everyone I could think of. I'm talking phone calls, emails, smoke signals! I personally connected with anyone who had commented or previously shown the least bit of interest in my workshops. Slowly, I started to book the seats. After a few weeks, we had reached the point where we had enough people committed to proceed with confidence. But still I persisted. Finally, just days before filming began, I sold the final spot. We were fully booked!

The event was a wild success, and my coaching career was on a new upward trajectory. It hadn't been easy—hey, if it were easy, everyone would do it—but I'd persevered!

Months later, I polled my group: How many times do you think I had to mention this workshop to book all thirty spots? The guesses ranged from a few times to maybe a dozen. Not even close. The reality was I had repeated my offer over a hundred times! So, don't worry that you'll wear people out or sound like a broken record.

When it comes to repetition, you almost can't overdo it. As long as you're creating a mix of personal and public invitations and serving from a place of authenticity, your tenacity will be rewarded.

This is a glimpse of your future.

Always remember, you have something incredible to bring into this world. When it comes to Connection Marketing, you must be your own most vocal advocate because no one believes in your business like you do! Marinate in the vision of success that you will create, not only for yourself but for your clients too. Once you have that vision in mind, go out and turn strangers into friends. Because you care about others, you owe it to them to help improve their lives. And the work you have done connecting will show you exactly where you are needed most. Invite those friends to come in. Drag them in if you must! Once they've experienced what you have to offer, they will be your next raving fans. Before you know it, the cycle you've set in motion will have your phone ringing and your invoices singing!

Now that you have some idea who your audience is, where to reach them, and how to invite them in, let's turn you into a sales expert!

7 | ON YOUR SIDE SELLING

One lazy summer afternoon, way back when I was just nine years old, a traveling salesman knocked on our door. This was halfway through summer break and the call of Super Mario World and trips to the local swimming hole were beginning to lose their allure. I was hard up for entertainment and this new fellow with a curious briefcase sparked my curiosity. I settled in at the kitchen table beside my mom to see what his presentation was all about.

From his case, he withdrew these curious objects: two tomatoes, a penny, a cutting board, a shiny knife, and a pair of scissors. I had to see where this was going. To start the show, the kindly salesman asked my mom if she wouldn't mind bringing her favorite cutting knife to the table. She obliged and he set to slicing. The first tomato dimpled and squashed as our family's trusty knife pressed into the flesh. A puddle of dripping seeds lay pulverized on the cutting board. Next up, with my mom's permission, he asked if I'd like to try *his* blade. Just like magic, the knife sliced through the second tomato. No mess. Just perfectly clean cuts. "Maybe you can help me out in the kitchen more," my mom ribbed.

The penny remained. What on earth was that for? The next trick blew my mind. His super shears sliced the penny clean in half! We tried to duplicate the feat with our scissors, but of course they never stood a chance.

"Mom! We *have* to get these!"

The show went on with more and more gadgets and knives and eventually the prices were presented too. Turns out the cost of the knife and the scissors alone were more than my mom brought in with a week of her substitute teacher pay—a lot to ask but a lot to gain! She pictured me at her side, or more likely my sister, the resident sous-chef. She imagined the ease of family meal prep and the promise of having a luxury tool at her fingertips. She bought into the idea of having a knife so durable she could hand it down to her kids and the proposed investment grew in value.

In the end, temptation won, and we were the proud new owners of a Cutco knife. The salesman shook my hand and left with a smile. To this day, that knife is still outperforming every blade in the block! Money well spent and a lifelong sales lesson well received.

The memory of that summertime sale shimmers with a golden glow. That day everyone at the table won. The salesman walked away with a new order, I got a great magic show, and my mom was sold a piece of her story—that she's a thoughtful homemaker with an eye for value. Above all, I learned that selling is fun, that trust and rapport seal the deal, and that both seller and buyer can win together when they're on the same side.

Meanwhile, Sara Blakely—founder of Spanx—was told a different tale. Early in her career, colleagues warned her that *business is war*. That startling insight rattled her to her core and made her question her approach. Would she join the crowd and subscribe to this masculine vision of sales as a battlefield? Or was there another way? Blakely chose to honor the feminine principles of collaboration and compassion and stay true to herself. That decision to trust her instincts and pursue business on her own terms paid off. She would go on to become the youngest female self-made billionaire.

There is no need to view sales as a competition between the seller and the buyer. My philosophy has always been one of inclusion and invitation. Let's join together on this! *Let's solve problems in harmony.* Instead of my client being on one side of the table and me on the other, it's both of us, side-by-side, making choices that bring shared wins. I succeed when she succeeds.

Put yourself in the client's shoes. What are *your* goals when you're considering a big investment? Who would you choose to serve your needs?

First, you want someone who's approachable and easy to get along with. Someone who listens to your concerns and can relate. You want a caring helper who appreciates and values your ideas.

Next, you also want someone who is an expert in her field. An experienced guide to take you through uncharted territory. You want to feel confident that you are in good hands. You need someone with authority that you can trust.

Throughout the sales process, you'll bring both of these traits—empathy and authority—to the table in equal measure.

Discovering Her Needs

Every sale starts with an inquiry. A client reaches out with a seemingly simple request: *I'm interested in your services. How*

TREAT EVERY LEAD LIKE GOLD.

much will this cost? By now you understand there is a story just beneath the surface. It's your job as a LUXE professional to dig a little deeper and find the need beneath the spoken need.

In my world, even a request as simple as, "How much for headshots?" has far too many variables for me to answer succinctly. *What kind of headshots are we talking about? Is this just a profile pic or a full personal branding portfolio? Will this be just you? You and your partner? Your entire office? What location did you have in mind? How many looks will you need?* The list goes on. My clients spend anywhere from $300 all the way up to $20,000 for this service, so providing a stab in the dark without all the information wouldn't be helpful. Neither would presenting a complicated price list and giving my prospect homework to try to decipher the options on her own. I owe it to both of us to take the time to understand her needs and develop the vision that will serve her best.

STEP ONE: PICK UP THE PHONE AND CONNECT.

Why the phone? Because written correspondence is inefficient and ineffective. As you'll see, the process we're launching requires close connection and a lengthy back-and-forth exchange. In order to properly read emotion, it's important to hear the nuance of tone. While texts and emails feel fast, they are slower than you think for communicating complex ideas. Plus, any client that's not willing to get on the phone likely isn't ready for the level of customization that you're offering, so think of this as a good way to screen them out.

Treat every lead like gold and respond as quickly as possible. If your call goes to voicemail, you're not off the hook. Leave a message and be prepared to follow up again. Here is a script that works like a charm to encourage your lead to call you back:

Thanks so much for reaching out! I want to hear all about what you have in mind for your upcoming project. I have a few questions for you so I can better understand your needs. Give me a call at 555-1212. Once I know more, I'll be able to tell you all about the products and services that will be perfect for you. Thanks! Look forward to hearing from you!

You've got the prospect on the phone. Now is the time to find out whether you're a good fit. As far as the quality of the sale is concerned, this is *the most* pivotal stage. After I've concluded a discovery call, I can usually project within a 10% margin of error where the final invoice total will land. That's how important this step is. Your work on this call sets the tone for the entire relationship.

Don't be surprised if the first question she asks is once again, "How much will this cost?" This doesn't necessarily mean she's price sensitive—it's just the first thing most people think to ask. You will definitely give her an answer, but first things first: You need to understand the scope of the project. Use this silver-bullet segue to put aside her pricing curiosity for now:

I'll be happy to answer that for you. But before I do, would it be alright if I ask you a couple questions so I can better understand your needs?

Boom! Just like that, you've been granted permission to dive deep into discovery questions.

STEP TWO: LEAD WITH EMPATHY.

In order to connect deeply, it's important that you first establish rapport. Remember the wisdom of Dale Carnegie: The more interest you show in others, the more they will feel bonded to you.

What are the right questions to ask during discovery? The more open-ended, the better. To show her that you understand and care, make it your goal in this phase to only talk 40% of the time and listen 60%. Give her the floor as much as possible and contribute to the conversation by adding brief statements that establish common ground. When a question sparks her interest and she starts to open up, pull on that thread. Be the guide and continue to ask additional questions to draw her out.

Here is a list of possible starters that may serve you well:

- *What is prompting you to do this now?*

- *What would success look like for you?*

- *Have you used a service like this in the past? Tell me about your experience. What went right? What do you wish had gone better?*

While you're listening, aim to uncover pain points and deeper concerns. Look for opportunities where your service could provide relief or solve a bigger problem.

- *What are you struggling with most at the moment?*

- *What would it mean to you to solve this?*

- *Who or what is standing in the way of your success?*

STEP THREE: BE THE AUTHORITY.

With the establishing questions settled, it's time to start hinting at solutions. Though it may be tempting to move into full presentation mode, don't hog the spotlight. Remain in the Q&A framework. Instead of *telling* her why you're the best option, ask leading questions that help her come to that determination on her own. If she's talking, she's engaged. The more you can keep her involved in the planning, the more ownership she will have in the process and outcome.

For example, I provide hair and makeup artistry at all portrait sessions. This differentiates me from most of my competition. I might pepper in a question like, "How important is it for you to look your best at the shoot?" My ideal client will of course answer: *very!* This provides me the opportunity to reply, "You are going to love our professional hair and makeup artist! She knows how to get you camera-ready and looking and feeling great! How would you like to wear your hair at the shoot?" I volley the question back to her so she can start daydreaming about how she will take advantage of this service I've just introduced. Just like that, I've sold her on one benefit of my elevated experience.

What is your x-factor? What makes your service special? Make a list of questions that will help guide your client to those conclusions. Only once your client has decided for herself that you have the best and most comprehensive solutions for her should you move on from this stage. Don't rush it. Your willingness to stay engaged and demonstrate your care and expertise will be your differentiator.[3]

STEP FOUR: SET UP THE CLOSE.

It's time to transition to logistics. We want to nudge the client out of her reverie and help her understand what it would take to make this dream a reality. I find this question most effective:

- *How soon are you looking to have this done?*

---

3 I once won a $10,000 office headshot bid—twice as much as my nearest competitor's proposal—because the head of marketing concluded, "No one's taken the time to understand our needs like you have! I'm putting your offer to the top of the stack." My key to success? Asking questions that helped her uncover solutions she craved.

Her answer will signal how serious and motivated she is to move forward. In addition, it will also provide you with crucial leverage later in the call to nudge her toward a "yes" decision.

While pegging down a date, consider the crowded restaurant theory. Let's say you have a choice between two places to eat. One is packed—the atmosphere is lively, the seats are full, and you can see there's a line of folks waiting for their chance to get in. The second is practically empty—the lights are on, but there's very little happening inside. Which one do you pick? If you're like most of us, you're subconsciously drawn to the place that's hopping. Without knowing any other details, you trust that the other patrons have good reason for having chosen the crowded restaurant.

This is the psychological phenomenon known as social proof. Humans are naturally drawn to follow the crowd. To help your clients understand your value, be the crowded restaurant. Even if your calendar is actually wide open, only offer her one or two dates to choose from. Rather than saying, "I'm free all afternoon. What time works best for you?" introduce a little scarcity: "I have an opening at 3:15 on Tuesday the 16th. Or if you prefer a time earlier in the day, I have 10:30am free on Thursday the 25th."

With a target date settled and all your preliminary questions answered, now is the time to present your vision. You'll give a brief recap of the conversation so far, and then pivot to the proposal you have in mind:

- *This is the problem you've described.*

- *This is the custom solution I have for you.*

- *This is (roughly) how much it will cost.*

When and How to Introduce Price

It's time to tell your client what lots she's on.

Let me explain what I mean by that. Say you're going to buy a car and you've got a budget of $35,000. First, you visit a Kia lot, and you learn that cars there cost between $10,000 and $40,000. With your budget, you can pretty much get whatever you want from Kia. Next you check out Lexus and discover the cars they sell run from $30,000 to $100,000. There are options for you on this lot too, but you'll have to stick to the lower end of what's available or increase your budget. Finally, you wander into a Rolls Royce dealership. Here, the prices start at $100,000 and go up from there. Whoa! Way too rich for your blood! You're definitely on the wrong lot now.

When we tell clients what lot they are on, we are giving them an opportunity to decide whether they've come to the right place. I like to say that I don't prequalify my clients; my clients prequalify themselves. If they have a Kia budget and find out you're a Rolls Royce dealer, they aren't going to hold it against you; they've just discovered that they're on the wrong lot. And even if you are a good match for them, knowing the full range of your prices will allow them to set their expectations. Can they afford any car on the premises, or just a base model?

When you present your price range, show them what's possible with a realistic entry point, but also don't be afraid to stretch to an ambitious number on the high end. This technique is called anchoring. A lot of customers would initially consider a $40,000 car to be expensive. But place that same car next to a premium model that costs $100,000 and they will see the $40k model in a whole new light. The high price is now an anchor in their mind, and they find great relief in having a significantly lower-priced option to consider.

The initial phone call is not the time to get stuck in the weeds with minor pricing specifics or what's included in which package. The opportunity for that level of detail will come later, when you're together in person. Our goals for the discovery call are to establish a relationship, convey a realistic price range, and get some buy-in before moving on to the next steps.

My typical price range reveal sounds like this: "We have some clients who purchase a handful of their favorite portraits and spend $1,500. We have other clients who say, 'I want to decorate every room in my home with wall art! I want a big, beautiful album, plus prints to share with friends and family.' They might end up spending $20,000 or more."

And then I tag on this pre-close question:

- *Does that sound like it will work for your taste and budget?*

At this point I'm looking for her reaction. Sometimes it's a confident, "Yes! That sounds perfect. Exactly what I had in mind!" Other times, it's a nervous joke, "Well, I'm not going to spend twenty thousand, I can tell you that much!" But whatever her response, I'm beginning to understand where she fits in the range. And so is she.

It's possible that she may need some time to think about it before committing. Maybe she needs to run it by someone else, or maybe she's decided she's not on the right lot and is looking for a polite way to decline. That's fine, but I always ask for permission to reconnect:

Let me do this. I want to make sure you don't lose your spot, so I'll put your date on hold until end of day tomorrow. Would it be all right if I follow up with you then to see where things stand?

Remember earlier when you and the client put a date on the calendar for your next meeting? This is where that step pays dividends. You've now introduced urgency and scarcity—*I can only hold this for you for twenty-four hours!* This motivates her to take action and removes her temptation to kick the decision down the road.

Assume the best and call back tomorrow with the hopeful expectation she'll be moving forward. If she ghosts you, you have your answer. But if she's good to go, ask her to affirm her commitment by collecting a deposit or down payment. This act of paying money will cement in the client's mind that the project has value to her. All you have to do is ask:

- *How would you like to pay for that?*

Ink these words onto your palm. Memorize them and use them every time. Having a go-to closing question like this will take away your fear and allow you to easily transition to the next step.

Completing the Vision

Your client has decided to move forward! Congratulations! Now let's talk about where your next interaction should take place. I recommend meeting clients in their home whenever possible.

Imagine your favorite celebrity chef. Just think how amazing it would be to experience a meal prepared by this artist. Now tell me, which would be more memorable: Eating at her restaurant or for her to prepare a private dinner at your home? Next consider a personal stylist. Which would impress you more? If she set aside a fitting room for you at your favorite department store or if she rolled up to your doorstep with a rack of curated options for you to try on in the comfort of your bedroom suite?

Home visits are the height of concierge service! Whenever possible, make your consultations easy and comfortable for your client by traveling to her. Serving clients out of state? You can still go to them through the power of Zoom and video conferencing.

The purpose of the in-person consultation is to meet the key players face-to-face and handle the details *for them*—take any measurements you need, confirm custom selections, and develop timelines. You'll have the opportunity to make a much more complete presentation than you ever could over the phone. You may arrive with visual aids, samples, and marketing collateral to show your client what's in store and increase her excitement for the finished project. Now is also the time to introduce any relevant pricing details. Be transparent and ready to answer all her questions. This is still a collaborative process, and you should listen closely to your client's feedback.

Throughout the sales process, you should always be on the lookout for opportunities to build value and further cement the relationship. Let me introduce a concept that social psychologists call the law of reciprocity. It states that whenever someone does something nice for us, we have a deep-rooted urge to do something nice in return. In fact, we often will reciprocate with a gesture far more generous than the original good deed. In sales, this means that unexpected treats or acts of service can be very powerful motivators.

Here's an example of reciprocity in action. For our twentieth anniversary, Aric and I chose to celebrate with an epic photo shoot in Florence and Venice, Italy. A bucket-list experience deserves a bucket-list photographer! My dream had long been to hire the legendary Jerry Ghionis. Having attended his photography workshops for years, I was completely sold that he was our guy, but since Aric didn't know him from Adam, he needed some convincing.

During our Zoom consultation, Jerry saw an opportunity to fire up that connection. In his endearing Australian accent, he turned to Aric and asked, "What are you gonna wear, mate?" When it came to wardrobe, I was all set. My vision was complete, right down to my shoes and accessories. But Aric desperately needed direction.

"Tell you what we could do," Jerry continued. "Why don't you just fly out to Vegas and we'll go shopping. I'll take you to all the best places and together we'll get this solved. Sound good?"

Las Vegas is home to Jerry's photography studio, not to mention some really great poker rooms. It was an easy yes for Aric. Shopping with a fashion-forward guide turned a necessary chore into a memorable adventure. It gave him the confidence that he'd look his best and eliminated a lot of unappealing homework. It also came with a distinct benefit for Jerry: the chance to build reciprocity. The truth is, the moment Aric agreed to the side trip, it sealed the deal on a five-figure portrait sale. That unexpected and generous offer by Jerry left us feeling generous in return. We would express our gratitude at the ordering appointment.

Reciprocity doesn't need to be this elaborate. Even an act as simple as bringing a chocolate or cup of coffee before presenting a restaurant bill can elicit higher tips. We use reciprocity in our portrait business by treating our clients to catered lunch on longer shoot days. We always pick up the check—our treat! Our clients' moods are lifted. They feel cared for and delighted. That $100 expense may translate to thousands of dollars on the back end as clients subconsciously express their thanks for the good feelings created.

RECIPROCITY DOESN'T **NEED** TO BE ELABORATE. EVEN **SMALL** GESTURES HAVE A **BIG** IMPACT.

Presenting the Invoice

Your client has hired you to make her life easier. She now trusts you as a caring expert who can solve her problems, and together you've worked out the parameters of the job at hand. It's time to get her final approval and collect payment. The keys to this step are confidence and clarity.

The fewer options you make her choose from, the better. Presenting a single comprehensive solution is best of all.

Always remember: You are not Subway!

At Subway restaurants, the customers are expected to make every decision. From the bread to the meat to all the toppings, it's basically a DIY experience. It doesn't matter who's behind the counter because they are only following directions. That's a fine model for a high-volume business operating in the value lane but remember that *you* are selling luxury.

Your business is more like a five-star restaurant, and you are the executive chef. Your client wants to hear your meal recommendation. And what's more, she expects that the ingredients, garnishes, and seasonings are all being handled. She'd probably appreciate a good wine pairing, too. You are expected to take care of all those details and make this a fantastic and memorable dining experience.

Here's an example of an invoice presentation gone wrong.

We recently ordered some custom window treatments for our home, and the decorator ran into trouble at the end of the sale. Her discovery call and initial in-home meeting had been smooth, and we were excited and ready to move forward. Suddenly and for no reason, she introduced complexity.

She emailed us three different invoices with prices ranging from $5,700 to $6,200. Considering how similar the totals were, we had to study the fine print to even figure out the differences between them. We noticed that one featured a nickel hardware finish and another white. One involved a curved curtain rod and another hinged. We had asked that the blinds open and close automatically on a timer, and curiously each invoice had a slightly different power option for the motor. To make matters worse, I found I wanted to mix and match. *Can I have the battery option from invoice three with the nickel finish from invoice two and the curved rod from invoice one? And actually, come to think of it, now I'm starting to wonder if I chose the right fabric. Should we backtrack and take a look at the samples again?* I was so confused, I wanted to start all over or maybe even cancel altogether.

In the words of Donald Miller, bestselling author of *Business Made Simple*, "When you confuse, you lose." What this designer should have done was listen to our feedback from the initial meeting, complete her product research, then present us with a *single* customized plan. We wanted an authority who could direct us confidently to a solution, not a sandwich artist.

Had I been presenting the invoice, it would have sounded like this:

Based on your home aesthetic, I recommend the custom curved rod with nickel finish. It will blend perfectly with your fabric choice noted here and beautifully complement your existing décor. I know you want to start your day waking up to the sunrise. I've tested several motors with timers and my clients find this model to be the most user-friendly and reliable. I've already lined up an electrician to join our team at installation,

135

CLIENTS WANT AN **AUTHORITY** WHO CAN DIRECT THEM **CONFIDENTLY** TO A **SOLUTION.**

and I'll also help you program the device to your preferred settings. Now all you need to do is relax and think about when you want to enjoy that beautiful view of yours! Here's the final invoice for everything we've discussed. How would you like to pay for that?"

Sold!

The Throw-Up Moment

Sometimes, I make my clients want to throw up. When this happens, it usually leads to my most impactful sales of all.

Let me explain.

I feel that a LUXE sales professional should always go for the gusto and put together the most comprehensive and ambitious proposal that she can. Don't just solve your client's presenting problem. Solve problems she didn't even consider. Keep expanding the scope. Whatever business you're in, the sale doesn't end until the client says stop.

As a result, sometimes after we've designed a truly audacious project together, I'll present an invoice so high that my client goes pale in the face, starts breathing deeply, and looks physically nauseous. When I see that reaction, I know I've done a good job.

Why on earth would I think that?

We've already learned that people attach value to things with high prices. When a client sees a total so scary that she needs to sit down, her decision to proceed anyway will become a defining moment in her life.

Think of it this way: If she didn't see the value in what you offered, it would be a trivial decision for her to decline. But since she really *does* want to realize that vision you've built up together, she now has to consider the very real possibility that she's about to pay an uncomfortable amount of money to move forward. She's being forced to decide just how important it is to own this piece of her story.

Give her the space to make that decision. After the final total has been revealed, there's no need for you to say anything else unless and until she voices an objection.

Big purchases involve big emotions. In my early years when I saw a sale creeping too high, my own insecurities would kick in and I'd try to "rescue" my client from spending too much. Even the tiniest moment of silence after I showed her the total would make me sweat. I would jump in to offer a discount or suggest places to make cuts.

Since then, I've worked hard to overcome my money blocks. Now when a client says, "Wow. That is a *lot* of money!" I just nod and smile and say in a carefree tone, "I know, right?" Keeping things light can go a long way toward diffusing tension. When I treat spending money as a joyful act, clients tend to follow my lead.

When her internal struggle finally ends and the decision is made to move forward, you now have a very committed client! One who has made the conscious decision to rewrite her story and shape her identity, seeing herself now as "the kind of person who..."

Think back to big purchases in your life. What is true for you?

- *I'm the kind of person who...values traveling the world.*
- *I'm the kind of person who...splurges on my family.*
- *I'm the kind of person who...spends big on education.*

YOU
ARE NOT
THE
PURSE
POLICE.

Going forward, she is now the kind of person who values the product or service you provide enough to pay dearly for it. Her desire to validate and celebrate her choice will make her your next raving fan.

If the client's decision, on the other hand, is that she just can't justify the big total, all is not lost. By making an ambitious initial offer, you've still given yourself room to concede. Take the invoice down to a fallback position. When we anchor clients by showing them a high price and then offer them a reprieve by showing a more affordable option, it becomes easier for them to say yes.

In addition to knowing where you can make concessions, you should also be prepared to offer thoughtful bonuses. All of my services have planned generosity built in. What that means is that I have anticipated where I can spoil my clients with upgrades they didn't see coming. People like savings, but they love rewards, too. Planning this in advance gives you leverage to seal the deal. Remember, your client wants to say yes. Throwing something in at the last minute gives her that final push and helps her understand you're on her side. She's spending more than she expected, but she's getting more, too!

Our aim is to build clients for life, so fairness and integrity are key. Be consistent. Think proactively about where and how you are willing to give a discount and a bonus, then universally make those offers for each client who qualifies.

In the end, we want our clients to feel good about the amount they've paid and the value they will receive. Our job is to challenge them, use psychology to make their decisions easier, and reassure them that they've made a great choice.

All that's left is to deliver on the grand vision you've built together!

WE'RE **NOT**
IN THE **BUSINESS**
OF SERVING
CUSTOMERS.
WE'RE IN THE
BUSINESS OF
BUILDING
CLIENTS
FOR **LIFE.**

8 | MAKE EVERY CLIENT HAPPY

I have been in business over a decade and in all that time, I've never had a bad review. My Google rating is a solid 5.0. Knowing this, you might expect that I turn out flawless experiences every time. But that's not the whole truth.

Listen, we are all human. We all make mistakes. Trust me! I could write a book about all the goofs and missteps I've had along the way. I've uttered some choice words and even shed some tears of frustration. Being an entrepreneur comes with high expectations and high emotions, and there will be moments where you just don't hit the mark...at least not on the first attempt.

The question is not *if* you will screw up, but *when.*

The mark of a truly exceptional business is how they perform in the trouble spots. When you struggle—when misunderstandings arise—will you fold your arms and stamp your feet? Or will you come back to the table and serve with your whole heart?

I don't know about you, but I simply won't accept letting my clients down. I will continue to have a five-star rating because of my philosophy: Never accept less than 100% satisfaction. Treating every client like a friend means going above and beyond to make things right.

Seeing Through Her Eyes

There are four words that can cut like a knife: *I'm disappointed in you.* One morning, I was woken up by an insistent series of 5:00 a.m. texts. I rolled over in bed, grabbed my phone, and as soon as my eyes caught sight of these words, my face flamed red. My client Jennifer must have had a sleepless night. The novella that followed expressed in no uncertain terms how angry she was that I had let her down.

My emotions turned from shame to anger. What had I done to deserve this wake-up tirade? Quite simply: I had missed the deadline on a delivery. She had been expecting her daughter's senior portraits to arrive before the weekend. And now here we were Monday morning—just days from the big graduation party—and she had "nothing to show for my $8,000 purchase!!" Two exclamation points. Never a good sign.

My first reaction was defensive. I mentally ran through a list of accusations myself. *Well, maybe if you had approved your album proof in a timely manner we wouldn't be in this position. Personal attacks flashed through my mind. Boo hoo, Jennifer! So sorry you won't have an album for your yacht party! Talk about First World problems!*

And then I took a deep breath and the good angel on my shoulder spoke up. *Well, she has a point.* I saw things through her eyes and imagined as a mother how stressed I would feel. This event was a big deal to her. It was a celebration of her only child gaining independence and the bittersweet moment when she'd leave the nest forever. She wanted everything to be just right so she'd spared no expense on the party or the album. And now she feared a massive part of her plans was in jeopardy. In her mind, I had disappointed her. She wasn't wrong.

A new emotion took over: empathy. I tuned into the situation. When I set aside my ego, I saw a friend who was hurting. The 5:00 a.m. texts. The double exclamation points. The long-winded note. There was a lot of emotion on display here. I was so caught up with the accusations that I had failed to see the question being asked: "Is there any chance we can get the album on time?"

I scurried to my computer and checked the tracking info. Turns out it was set to be delivered that very day. The weekend had made it seem like I was three days late, but really, I was only one business day behind. I had broken the cardinal sales rule: Always *under*promise and *over*deliver. If I had just pushed my estimate out a few days, we wouldn't be in this pickle. But because I had set her expectation for Friday, she was now counting every late hour as a demerit in her book.

I set the phone aside and laced up my shoes for a walk. *How could I make this right?* The first thing was to reassure her that everything was fine. But I wanted to do more. The surface problem—order delivery—was easy to fix, but the deeper issue—broken trust—needed to be salved. I decided to go the extra mile. Before heading off to my morning meetings, I ordered up a bouquet of flowers and had it rushed to her home. Along with the flowers went a note of sincere apology and these simple words: "You deserve more, Jennifer."

At noon I got a call from her number. But no one was speaking. *Had she misdialed me? Was I still in trouble?* There was a hitch of breath and then I heard it. She was crying. "Jennifer, are you okay?"

"I'm so sorry. I thought I had it together before I called you."

"No, no, you're totally fine. I'm glad you called. I wanted to tell you..."

She interrupted me. "Megan, you don't owe me any apologies. I'm sitting at my kitchen table looking at the most beautiful pictures I've ever seen. The album arrived this morning. What I wasn't expecting was these flowers. And the note..."

And here she lost it again.

I gave her space to compose herself. "I just realized, with the divorce and all..."—*Oh yeah! She had hinted at a rough divorce!*—"... do you know that I can't remember that last time someone said, 'I'm sorry?' What you've done today means everything. I didn't realize how much I needed this."

You never know what people are going through. Clearly, being one business day late was not the end of the world. It was a misstep and a disappointment to be sure. But beyond that, it was a symbol of all that was out of her control and proved to Jennifer that people would keep letting her down, that no one cared about her needs. She felt alone, stressed, and overwhelmed. And it was that storyline that she would suffer no longer.

One kind and generous action was all she needed to restore her hope in the world. Jennifer did deserve more! And I am overjoyed that I could help her write a new story that day. Her trust in me was repaired, and she became another delighted customer.

WHEN SOMEONE **OVERREACTS** TO A PROBLEM, DON'T TAKE IT **PERSONALLY.** YOU **NEVER** KNOW WHAT **PEOPLE** ARE **GOING** THROUGH.

What a difference we can make in the lives of our clients! And what did it take from me? Understanding. Humility. Compassion. I bring my empathy advantage to work every day.

Conversations, Not Contracts

Most conflicts can be boiled down to one simple problem: faulty communication. Luxury clients want and deserve a lot of hand holding. They don't like feeling confused. And for important matters, nothing beats verbal communication. Providing quick text reminders or email checklists is fine, but you should assume that *no one actually reads anything*. Explaining things aloud to your client will help her feel connected and at ease. Be sure to make eye contact and always check for confirmation that you're on the same page.

A lengthy project is like miles of dark, twisty road. In order to reach your destination, it's not necessary to memorize every turn up front—you just need enough visibility to keep steering through the next bend. In the same way, you should turn on the headlights for your client at each step. Never leave her wondering what's happening next, but also don't burden her with too much information before she needs it. She will appreciate a well-defined process and the feeling that she's in good hands. If your client is confused, don't get frustrated at her for not following instructions. Examine your own process to figure out how you can make things better for her and improve for the future.

In my observation, a lot of small businesses are relying too heavily on contracts to do their communicating for them. Sometimes they assume (or have been told) that's just the way business is done. Often, it's because they've had clients act "the wrong way" in the past, and they're trying to force future ones into line. It's a natural reaction; they've been hurt before and figure this will be an easy fix. But remember, their clients are probably not going to read that agreement, so the problem will occur again. And now there will be a document forcing both sides into an awkward and adversarial position. That's the opposite of "on your side" selling.

Obviously, there are valid situations where a contract is necessary. If the stakes of a transaction are high enough that you could see one party suing the other, by all means get that agreement in writing! Building a home, hosting a conference, selling a car...in any situation where tens of thousands of dollars are on the line or there's only one chance to get something right, a legal agreement may be warranted. On the other hand, if you're just using a contract as a way to direct your client's behavior, you may be better off replacing that document with a conversation.

Let me give you a few examples from my own industry. If I were hired to shoot a wedding, I'd probably have a contract drawn up. It's a unique event and the stakes are high. Photographers have been sued before by unhappy brides. I'd want a contract for my own protection in the event of trouble, and to make sure expectations were clear on both sides before that emotional day arrived.

On the flip side, I don't need to bring a contract in on more routine shoots like office headshots, a boudoir session, or family portraits. If things don't go as planned, I can always make it right with a reshoot. Or, worst case scenario, I can simply offer a refund. I'm not concerned about being sued by my client over a small job like this. And since I'd never in a million years take her to court, I don't see the need to bring pen and paper into the equation. To make matters right, we simply need to talk things over and a resolution can be reached.

TURN ON THE HEADLIGHTS FOR YOUR CLIENT AT EACH STEP.

If I see a problem happen once, I chalk it up as a one-off. If that same issue happens again, I raise an eyebrow and get curious. When I see it happen three times? Well, now I know there's a pattern. It's time to roll up my sleeves and unearth the root of the problem.

To paraphrase Nelson Mandela: I never lose. Either I win or I learn. Every time something has gone wrong in my business, I retrace my steps and identify the moments where I could have done better. This is an opportunity for me to correct my process for the future.

In my second year in business, I started seeing a rash of clients rescheduling shoots at the last minute. This was causing a real problem for me. I had reserved the day, lined up hair and makeup artists, and sometimes even arranged catered lunches. I checked in with some professional photography forums for advice and got a lot of, "Well what does your contract say?" and "Did she sign a contract? Charge your reschedule fee!" These contract crusaders saw everything as You vs. Me, and they weren't about to back down from a misbehaving client.

I didn't agree with such punitive measures. Rather than squabbling with people over penalty charges, I decided to investigate. Why were these clients rescheduling in the first place? After some reflection and time spent putting myself in their shoes, I came up with an answer: They simply felt overwhelmed. A lot of my clients had put off the question of what to wear until it was too late. Rescheduling or canceling was a huge relief for them because they didn't feel ready. Looking at it another way, I hadn't done enough to help them prepare.

As soon as I realized this flaw in my process, I set out to correct it. That's when I introduced "Style and Concept Consultations." Going forward, I'd meet every client in the comfort of her home to discuss her goals. We'd solve her what-to-wear problems by picking out her clothes and accessories together. I would also use this time to meet everyone who would be at the shoot, go over my pricing in detail, and show them product samples. This extra point of contact went a long way toward building everyone's trust and excitement for the big day. They wouldn't back out on me now because not only did they feel prepared, but I was now their friend.

Just like that, my reschedules and cancellations dropped back to a rarity. What's more, my average sale started to creep upward as I was able to use these in-home visits to scout out locations for wall art installations. While the folks in the forums were waving their contracts in the air and squabbling over reschedule fees and credit card chargebacks, I was over here solving problems in a LUXE way.

No One Is the Villain in Her Own Story

When I studied theater in college, one lesson really stuck with me. My director taught us that no character ever sees themself as the villain. Everyone's actions are justified by their history, beliefs, and present circumstances. Any time you stop to consider your character's true motivation, you can begin to see why they act and react in a certain way.

It's the same with your clients. Whatever demands they're making, whatever attitude they're copping, they are acting in a manner that seems reasonable and justified to them at that moment. Your job is to figure out their motivation and only react once you have that understanding.

I have a mantra I say whenever I find a client challenging:

There is nothing you can do or say that will make me love you less.

I NEVER LOSE. EITHER I WIN OR I LEARN.

SKIP THE PENALTIES AND SOLVE THE ROOT PROBLEM INSTEAD.

When a client is being difficult, tune in to her even more deeply. Imagine how you would treat her if she were your mother, sister, or best friend. Think of how *you'd* like to be approached if you were wrestling with her worries and insecurities. With a little strategy, you can put out this fire. And more than that, by solving her problem in an empathetic way, you have an incredible opportunity to turn her into one of your strongest evangelists.

In the ten steps below, I'll guide you through my surefire strategy of negotiation and conflict resolution. Here's how I would go about changing her heart and mind.

Step 1: Walk away. Do not respond to that angry text or email right now. Take a breather. Talk it over with a trusted friend or mentor. Sleep on it. There is no need to add fuel to the fire by responding in anger. Do whatever you need to do to arrive at a balanced, problem-solving mindset.

Step 2: See with eyes of empathy. Remember, no character thinks she's the villain. She's having a problem and trying to get her needs met. She wants you to present a solution. Granted, the way she is asking you to solve it may not seem fair to you. But if you can put yourself in her shoes and find her motivation for acting this way, you'll be better able to help.

Step 3: Consider where *you* went wrong. Acknowledge that you are partly to blame for the misunderstanding. Identify the stage in your process where you faltered. Did you make assumptions that turned out to be wrong? Was there a lack of communication? Did you take a shortcut or skip over a vital step?

Be prepared to say you're sorry in a real and authentic way. No *I'm-sorry-buts* allowed. Simply, "I'm sorry I let you down." Or, as we saw in the opening example, "You deserve better." People are

THERE IS **NOTHING** YOU **CAN** **DO** OR SAY THAT WILL MAKE ME **LOVE** YOU **LESS.**

so used to inauthentic, meaningless apologies that they will be overwhelmed with gratitude to see you setting things right. When you bend in cooperation, yielding to the attack, the blows soften. Think of it as apology aikido—harmonizing with your attacker rather than resisting them.

Step 4: Identify where you are willing to compromise. Are there things you can do to show your client you care? Are there any bonuses you can extend that would smooth over the problem?

Alternately, where will you *not* compromise? What concessions would violate the integrity of your business? When I feel I am being pulled beyond my comfort zone, I use this line: "In fairness to my other clients, I can't do that." Of course, be ready with a counterproposal. "While I won't be able to do that, I could do this...." Solving problems through compromise means both sides give a little, but it can still feel like a win-win.

Step 5: Rehearse the problem-solving conversation. How will the conversation unfold? What curveballs might come up? Mentally practice before you reach out. Role playing with a friend or mentor is a great way to be prepared. I like to practice by taking situations to the extreme. When you prepare for a client at rage level ten and then discover she's only throwing rage level five at you, it's actually quite a relief!

Step 6: Call the client. Yes! *Call.* Promise me you won't email or text. If you have truly engaged with the steps above, I promise you will be ready. As for your client, she may *not* be. At least, not right away. If your call goes to voicemail (which it likely will) assume that she is not picking up because she needs space. Be prepared with a voicemail script that invites her to return the call.

157

Hi there! I've been thinking about what you said, and I want you to know I am on your side. I know we can make this right and find a fair solution for you and me. I've got a couple ideas to help solve the problem. Give me a call and we'll talk it over. Look forward to hearing from you!

Step 7: Engage with empathy. When you do get her on the phone, start with a tension reliever, the "I am on your side" line from above. After this opener, acknowledge what you did wrong. Throw yourself under the bus. Be humble and human. Owning up to your mistakes can be very disarming for a client and it invites them to react with empathy, too. Never point a finger at what *she* did wrong (or what you perceive she did wrong). Remember: she does not think of herself as the villain, and you should know that by now from your soul-searching walk in her shoes. It may be helpful to name the emotion and problem you've identified she's wrestling with. This will further help her understand that you're on her side.

What not to say: "Unfortunately, you didn't read the contract. If you did, you would have known that..."

What to say instead: "I realize now that I forgot to share the prices and process aloud with you. I apologize for this oversight. No wonder you were taken aback! I can imagine how stressed I'd feel if I were in your shoes and learning these details last minute."

Step 8: Propose a solution. What did you identify as a possible compromise? This is where you'll share your plan. Check for buy-in by asking a closing question, such as: "Would that work for you?" or "Can we move forward and give that plan a try?" Only after you hear an affirmation should you move forward. If the client does not agree to what you've just said, this is her time to voice that concern.

Step 9: Listen deeply. Act fairly. If your closing question leads to rejection, don't panic. Listen and listen well. She will provide you with course correction information showing you where you misunderstood her point of view and needs. I like to have a pen and paper handy and highlight key words and ideas. This keeps me focused on her and gives me room to digest her words.

If you can propose a counter-solution on the fly, do so. If, however, you are blindsided and feel that same panic and anger you did before you started this process, take another breather. Don't speak in anger; use this phrase instead: "You've brought up a new point—something I hadn't thought of. Let me take a moment to consider this. Can we reconnect later this evening?"

Step 10: Follow up and follow through. Walk the talk and make sure you follow through on what you said you'd do for the client. Check in at the conclusion with the simple question, "Does everything meet your expectations?" Thank her for working with you and for her purchase. Another satisfied client!

Problem solving in this way is an extremely valuable skill that will help you rise to the top in all your business interactions. And don't forget, while a lot of this chapter has been focused on the times things go wrong, most of your clients will be delighted and delightful from beginning to end!

Let's put a final coda on our sales process with...

The Victory Lap

That's a wrap! Your work together has concluded. You have a fully satisfied client and, even better, you have a brand cheerleader and a new friend!

My victory lap comes during the wall art installation. My client is seeing her beautiful printed images for the first time, and I'm taking all her homework away by installing them in her home. We spend time chatting, recalling fun moments we had, and admiring how amazing everything looks on her walls. Just like we planned.

I'm also planting the seeds for future projects where I can. Asking permission to celebrate her work on my business pages, nudging her to leave me an online review, or following up on a referral lead she mentioned in one of our earlier conversations.

The main point is: the victory lap is a great time to just hang out with your client for a moment and bask in what you've accomplished together. The invoice is paid, the service is delivered, everyone is relaxed and happy.

Through it all, you've been on the same side. You've served up your best, creating not just an exceptional experience but also a friendship. Just because the project is behind you doesn't mean the relationship ends here. Next time your client needs your services, there's no doubt who she'll call.

You're a piece of her story now.

CONCLUSION: START BEFORE YOU'RE READY

Just today, two new students joined the ranks of the $10k Club. Another texted me to report, "It's really happening! Clients are paying thousands...and *thanking* me for the opportunity!" In big cities and small towns all over the United States and the world, small business owners are growing into breadwinners, clients are happier than ever, and dreams are becoming reality.

Want to join the ranks of the highest achievers? Let me fill you in on our little secret. No one was 100% ready before they launched. We all started a little unsure. Remember the question from the beginning of the book? That crazy idea of tripling your prices might have sent you into a tailspin of dread. But now, armed with new information, confidence, and resolve, you might find you're ready for the challenge...and then some! In fact, if you're not feeling the least bit nervous, I would say your dreams aren't big enough. Go back to the drawing board and sketch out something even more audacious!

You picked up this book because you have a calling. Don't let excuses or perfectionism stop you. Use the resource you have in your hands and take your first step forward.

Set up your pricing and process. Get your head in the game and then go serve your first client, even if you have to drag them in. You can always improve things later. In fact, if you're like me, you'll never stop improving.

Get out there and build the business and the life of your dreams! Start today!

ACKNOWLEDGMENTS

Behind every great woman is a great man. And my great man Aric has been my rock through this all. My Lew, thank you for all the stories we have created together over twenty-one years. Thank you for every act of service, every supportive word, and yes, thank you even for the battles. This book is perfect and perfectly ours because of all the time you spent shaping it with me. Everything is better in my life and in our businesses because of you. I can't wait to see how our next chapters will unfold.

I am a strong woman because of the strong woman that raised me. Mom, when you were a girl, you were told there were just three options for your future: homemaker, nurse, or teacher. You were determined to show your children and your students that our futures are what we choose. Though it must have felt scary and unfamiliar, you supported every new move my business took and every new calculated risk. You gave me space to fail, and you gave me encouragement when I needed it most. I never would have finished this book without your constant cheerleading. My deepest thanks to you and Dad for loving me and believing in me.

Koan and Veda, you introduced me to my passion for photography. I can never get enough pictures of you! Art runs in our family. I am constantly inspired by your creativity and independence. You two have become such fine young adults and I'm proud to be your mom. What I love most of all is how you both exemplify empathy, compassion, and kindness in all you do! I do believe you and your generation will change the world for the better.

To my writing coach, Derek Lewis, thank you for your guidance and your friendship throughout the process. It was so great to have a role model and a connector like you to show us the way. I appreciate all the time and care you shared with us on this journey!

Where would I be without my team members and friends? Jessi Norvell, you are an absolute gift to me and the Megan DiPiero Photography brand. You put empathy in action every day. You are a true leader who inspires the heck out of me and lifts up our clients and our industry. Tamara Knight, you have been my truest and longest friend. You are the caring confidante who gave me courage when I needed it most. Thank you both for believing in my message and sharing it with our coaching community.

Special thanks to all our Rise to the Top members! In our Facebook group, you'll often hear: "What Would Megan Do?" You all make me ask more of myself. I am a better leader because of you. When I see a student take the lessons and run with them, I am inspired to give more. We are changing the industry together! We are changing lives together.

And finally, to my clients…I love being a part of your lives! Thank you for letting me in as a friend. I have a mission to empower women through portraits and business makeovers. I step up to the plate to serve every day. But I couldn't be at my best if it weren't for the trust you placed in me. Thank you for the leap of faith you took—for moving forward and embracing your worth. I am honored to be a part of your story.

ABOUT THE AUTHOR

Megan DiPiero is a world-renowned business coach who has helped thousands of entrepreneurs achieve breadwinner status and six-figure incomes. She is the owner of several companies including Megan DiPiero Photography, Megan DiPiero Coaching, and Frame-Suite. Through her sales workshops and coaching community, Megan inspires business owners to elevate their game and make money that matters. She lives in sunny Southwest Florida with her husband and business partner, Aric, and their two resident artist children. Together they love traveling the world, meeting her students and building empires.

DOWNLOADS

For bonus materials and downloadable versions of the
worksheets printed in this book, please visit:
SheSellsBook.com/Resources

———————

COACHING

For more information on Megan's workshops and
upcoming speaking engagements, please visit her website:
MeganDiPieroCoaching.com

———————

PHOTOGRAPHERS

Are you a professional photographer or aspiring pro?
Join the conversation in our uplifting and educational
Facebook forum: Rise to the Top! with Megan DiPiero
Facebook.com/groups/RisetotheTopwithMeganDiPiero

Printed in Great Britain
by Amazon

67073475R00102